SHADOWS OF

OF

WEST YORKSHIRE

Keith A. Jenkinson

An Autobus Review Publication

ISBN 0 907834 20 5

First published August 1990

Previous page : Turning the clock full circle, red buses once again operate to the Bradford suburb of Clayton after an absence of almost sixty years, albeit now by Yorkshire Rider who occasionally employ former West Yorkshire Bristol VRTs and Olympians on their 636/7 routes. During the late 'twenties/early 'thirties Clayton was served by Blythe & Berwick who were purchased by West Yorkshire in 1928. Here Tilling red & cream liveried 746 is pictured at Lidget Green on 28 June 1990.

Front cover upper : Yorkshire Rider 744, a former West Yorkshire Road Car Co.Ltd. Bristol VRT was unique in being the only bus other than the ex.Sovereign Bus & Coach Atlanteans to receive its new owner's colours but retain West Yorkshire fleet names. It is seen here approaching Bradford's Interchange at the end of its journey from Leeds on the 670 service on 2 April 1990.

Front cover lower : Keighley & District adopted a new, and somewhat uninspiring, livery of chinchilla & red in the autumn of 1989. One of the first vehicles to be repainted into these new colours was short Leyland National 1016 which is seen here collecting its Riddlesden-bound passengers in Keighley bus station whilst working local service 708 on 11 October 1989.

Typeset by Autobus Review Publications Ltd.

Printed by Icon Impressions Ltd.,Bacup, Lancashire.

Autobus Review Publications Ltd., 42 Coniston Avenue, Queensbury, Bradford BD13 2JD.

INTRODUCTION
&
ACKNOWLEDGEMENTS

Since the publication of 'Northern Rose' which traced the history of West Yorkshire Road Car Co. Ltd. from its foundations in 1906 up to its return to the private sector from the National Bus Company, more than was ever imagined has taken place with the result that this once-great company has, in the space of less than three years, almost disappeared.

West Yorkshire's new owners have not only restructured themselves - several times - but have also restructured the operating company, divided it and finally sold more than half its buses and operations. Of this once great empire, only the parts in and around Keighley, Grassington and Harrogate now survive and it appears doubtful that the latter will survive in the hands of its present owners for many more months.

What then has happened to West Yorkshire Road Car Co. Ltd. since August 1987 ? Within the following pages an attempt has been made to record the numerous changes that have taken place up to and after the demise of this former Tilling / NBC company and with a combination of text and photographs the story unfolds as the various events took place.

Although much of the content has been drawn from my own recordings and observations, I would express my thanks to the West Yorkshire Information Service whose monthly news-sheet have confirmed numerous details and have provided additional information. All the photographs included in the following pages are by the author except where credited otherwise.

Despite this book covering such a short period of time, it was felt that changes of such magnitude should be recorded sooner rather than later and I hope readers will find the following pages as interesting to read as I did to write.

Keith A. Jenkinson,
Queensbury,
Bradford.

July 1990

Top : Keighley & District dual purpose-seated Leyland Olympian 69 has yet to receive its owner's new chinchilla & red livery as it approaches Bradford Interchange in June 1990.

Above : Although wearing an all-over advertising livery for the Museum of Automata, York City & District's Pheonix-bodied Iveco minibus 211 retained its normal cream & blue colours at the front. It is seen here in Station Rise, York on 2 June 1990 enroute to Woodthorpe on city service 3.

Below : Resting in Templar Street, outside Vicar Lane bus station, Leeds in pre-Yorkshire Rider days is West Yorkshire Leyland National 1492. New in October 1979 it passed to Yorkshire Rider in August 1989 and was soon afterwards renumbered 1337.

THE BEGINNING OF A NEW DAWN

Taking up the history of West Yorkshire Road Car Co.Ltd. at the time of its return to the private sector after forty years under state control, it might be appropriate to firstly recap on the events which led to its departure from the National Bus Company fold. Following the passage of the 1985 Transport Act under which it was announced that all the National Bus Company subsidiaries were to be privatised before 1988, West Yorkshire's senior management team under the leadership of Giles Fearnley, the company's Financial Director, set about drawing up plans for the bid they were to submit to the Department of Transport in their attempt to gain control of their company. In the meantime however, competitive bids were being prepared by several other companies interested in acquiring West Yorkshire Road Car Co. Ltd. and amongst these were Stagecoach of Perth; Carlton PSV Sales; bus & coach dealer Stuart Johnson and United Transport International, and from the start it appeared that the company's management team had a battle on their hands.

Following the submission of bids from the various interested parties, the wait began for the Department of Transport's decision and unusually, before this was given, the National Bus Company took the unusual step of announcing their recommendation before the transaction had been completed. The reason for this break in tradition was that the bid being recommended to the Department of Transport was very different to any that had previously been submitted for the acquisition of other NBC companies. The bid concerned was led by Alan J. Stephenson who was joined by three members of West Yorkshire's present management team - Giles Fearnley, Andrew Guest and Tom Fox and also included the involvement of Leeds-based development company Parkdale Holdings plc. It was because of Parkdale's inclusion that an early announcement was made as it was necessary for them to inform the Stock Exchange of their intentions at the earliest opportunity before it then sought the approval of its shareholders. Alan Stephenson was no stranger to West Yorkshire, having served as Secretary of the company from 1977 until 1985 when he left to take up the position of General Manager of East Yorkshire Motor Services Ltd. at Hull. Already being part of the management team who had purchased the latter company from the NBC raised questions regarding potential conflict of interest between that company and West Yorkshire due to their sharing of common boundaries in part of North Yorkshire. Despite previous statements by the NBC that they would not allow adjacent companies to be acquired by the same buyer, they felt that on this occasion there would be no such conflict of interest, a point not welcomed or readily accepted by West Yorkshire PTA who had been refused the opportunity to bid for West Yorkshire on the grounds that such a move would be anti-competitive.

Following the approval of Parkdale Holdings' shareholders to that company's involvement in the bid, the Secretary of State fot Transport finally announced his acceptance to the joint Management/Parkdale acquisition of West Yorkshire Road Car Co.Ltd. on 23 July 1987, the completion of the sale taking place a month later on 25 August. Under the agreement, Parkdale Holdings plc acquired all the properties at that time vested in the company and gave an undertaking to the NBC that it would lease back to West Yorkshire all of those properties that it needed for the running of its business. The fleet and operations of the former NBC subsidiary passed to Alan Stephenson and the company's senior management team under the leadership of Giles Fearnley who had taken up the position of Managing Director on 1 August following the previous occupant of this post, Brian Horner's earlier decision to leave the company. West Yorkshire Road Car Co. Ltd. thus became the 44th subsidiary of the National Bus Company to be privatised.

At first, few changes were to be seen as a result of of the company's change of ownership, although as was to be expected, speculation was rife as to what the future might hold. In the interim period, the eradication of the Citibus fleetname at York was completed during the week commencing 17 August when the final vehicles to carry this received white-lettered West Yorkshire vinyl fleet names. The now-common service revisions following de-regulation continued unabated, and the first casualties of the new era were the 650/2 and X65/6 routes which on 13 September were truncated to terminate at Ilkley rather than continue the mile or so further to Ben Rhydding which was already served by the company's local minibus routes. During the following month, West Yorkshire gained the contract to provide the free bus services to the Asda supermarket at Pudsey previously operated by Baildon Motors and for this purpose transferred two short Leyland Nationals from Harrogate to Leeds depot, these being the first of their type to be allocated to the latter. More dramatically however, York independent Reynard Pullman secured a 3-year contract from York City Council for the operation of the 14 and 14A services from Piccadilly to Elmfield Avenue previously operated by West Yorkshire. Commencing on 26 October, this gave Pullman their first major foothold on local services in the city and although not known at that time, this whet their appetite for further expansion in future years.

Having now dispensed with its York Citibus name and image, it came as something of a surprise when on 4 November West Yorkshire announced a new identity for its York-based fleet, this being York City & District. This new operation was to be managed by Nigel Jolliffe who had previously been West Yorkshire's Business Development Manager, and in its press release York City & District promised cleaner buses; the scrapping of the exact fares policy and the replacement of fare boxes and old ticket machines with new electronic equipment. The new fleet name was immediately applied to all buses operating in the York fleet and was also added to publicity material etc. as this was reprinted.

York City & District at one time operated a large fleet of Bristol VRT double deckers. One of these, 1738 picks up its passengers opposite York railway station on a cold March day in 1989. (J.Whitmore)

As had been expected, connections between Alan Stephenson's two interests, West Yorkshire Road Car Co. Ltd. and East Yorkshire Motor Services Ltd. began to develop and in October, following the acquisition of Hardwicks of Scarborough by the latter on the 5th of that month, a trio of West Yorkshire Plaxton Paramount-bodied Leyland Tiger coaches were despatched to Scarborough on loan to Hardwicks to assist them over a temporary vehicle shortage. They eventually returned to their rightful owner in mid November. Meanwhile, Bristol Lodekka driver training bus 4068 during September underwent a repaint from NBC poppy red to West Yorkshire's smart Tilling red & cream livery. Immediately before its fleet name transfers were applied however, instructions were received that it was instead to be painted all-over white, and so it was thus transformed to become the first - and only - Lodekka in the fleet to gain this uninspiring colour scheme.

One of the four Robin Hood-bodied Iveco minibuses acquired from Southdown, 158 (D115DRV) like its sisters began life with People's Provincial at Gosport. Painted in standard West Yorkshire Hoppa livery, it is seen here in Knaresborough on 21 June 1989.

After being repainted into Tilling red & cream livery, driver training Bristol FS6B Lodekka MWW114D was immediately repainted all-over white as seen here at Rougier Street, York on 1 December 1987. Happily, none of the other Lodekka driver tuition buses were subjected to this uninspiring paint style.

The need for additional minibuses led West Yorkshire to purchase four Robin Hood-bodied Iveco 49.10s from Southdown Motor Services during mid-October. Being almost identical to those already operated by the company, this quartet had originally started life with People's Provincial at Gosport before moving to Southdown, and after being repainted into West Yorkshire's blue Hoppa livery and being given fleet numbers 158-61, two entered service at Harrogate on 26 October with the remaining pair taking up their duties on the first day of the following month.

Numerous service changes were implemented during November and a new once daily operation was introduced between Rougier Street, York and Gallowgate coach station, Newcastle upon Tyne. Numbered 490 and commencing on 12 November, this operated only on Thursdays, Fridays and Saturdays. Hail and Ride facilities were added to Otley's two minibus-operated town services at the beginning of the month, but more importantly, on 2 November West Yorkshire lost their daytime operations on the X1 limited stop service from Bradford to Otley via Leeds/Bradford Airport to Rhodes Coaches of Yeadon who on this occasion were the victors under the tendering procedure. Prior to this, on 26 October in Keighley, the 716 service was extended to run to Morrison's supermarket and was marketed as the Shann Hoppa whilst a new service (713) was introduced from Silsden to Morrisons in Keighley under the title Silsden Hoppa.

Twenty surplus Leyland Nationals which had spent several months in store in the non-operational depot at Ilkley were eventually sold on 28 October to Martins (dealers) of Middlewich whilst during the following month, an ECW-

bodied Leyland Olympian received fixed glazing to its nearside front upper deck bulkhead window, thus giving it a 'winking' appearance. This was to result in numerous Olympians having their troublesome opening-type front upper deck bulkhead windows replaced by fixed glazing in the months (and years) ahead in an attempt to resolve the problems associated with the former.

The first full-sized vehicles to be purchased new by the company since its return to the private sector arrived at Harrogate on 10 December in the form of two Leyland Lynx single deckers which sported a new predominantly cream livery with red relief and a new-style fleet name. Within two days, both buses were to be seen on driver familiarisation duties and a couple of days later they entered service on the Harrogate to Knaresborough corridor, adorned internally with balloons and streamers in celebration of the festive season. As an additional novelty, many of the drivers of these two buses dressed up in Santa Claus outfits, a feature which appealed to young and old alike. In order to improve the quality of the vehicles used on the company's longer stage carriage services and particularly the prestigious 36 route from Leeds to Ripon via Harrogate, Leyland Olympian 1846 had its bus-type seating replaced by coach seats, and after being repainted into a predominantly cream livery with red relief similar to that worn by the new Lynxes, it re-entered service in its new form on 18 December. Three days prior to

Rhodes Coaches of Yeadon gained the tender for the Bradford - Otley via Leeds/Bradford Airport X1 service previously operated by West Yorkshire. 26BMR, a Plaxton-bodied Leyland Leopard with a windscreen-mounted destination board climbs out of Bradford enroute to Otley on 28 April 1988.

this, another Olympian (1815) was despatched to Leeds coachbuilders Optare where it was to receive similar treatment and it was planned that a total of 12 buses of this type were to be thus modified.

Before 1987 ended, the company's enquiry and booking office in Skipton was offered for sale, the business being continued from new premises nearer to the town's bus station.

A new year dawned and brought with it the arrival in January of 20 new Robin Hood-bodied 23-seat Iveco 49.10 minibuses. Unlike the company's previous Hoppas which carried a blue livery, these new additions to the fleet were painted cream & red and the two allocated to Keighley depot (165/78) were given Keighley Hoppa fleet names. The remainder were unlettered and although all were specified with automatic transmission, the first two received were fitted with manual gearboxes. Both were eventually returned to their manufacturer for the retrospective fitting of automatic transmission to bring them into line with their sisters. Towards the end of the month, a further 12 surplus Leyland Nationals left the fleet upon their sale to Martins (dealers) of Middlewhich and were joined by a pair of Bristol VRT driver training vehicles which had been unused since December 1986. As a result of the introduction by the Department of Transport on 1 January of a new taxation class for recovery vehicles which prohibited these from being operated on trade plates, the company had to register all their vehicles of this type with conventional numbers, thus breaking a long-standing tradition.

A new minibus service from Otley to Ilkley (numbered W5) was inaugurated on 3 January whilst a week later, Pinnacle Coaches of Crosshills further encroached on the company's territory by starting a new service from Ilkley to Skipton via Steeton. Across in York, the first of the promises made by York City & District materialised on 24 January when that

depot's Almex ticket machines and fare boxes were replaced by a new Wayfarer electronic ticketing system and several services were revised to take account of passenger's needs.

Following the collapse of negotiations relating to the acquisition of Premier Travel, Cambridge by Cambus, Alan Stephenson and Giles Fearnley, together with West Yorkshire Investments Ltd. on 10 February joined forces with Premier's management and purchased that company. Although there was no intention of bringing Premier into the West Yorkshire fold and the Cambridge-based company was to retain its autonomy, it seemed more than likely that some form of link would eventually be established between West Yorkshire and Premier. This was soon confirmed when a pair of West Yorkshire Plaxton-bodied dual purpose Leyland Leopards were despatched on loan to Premier for whom they operated for a couple of weeks.

The next changes to be witnessed took place in February when, in an attempt to attract more passengers and to compete more vigorously with their rival, Challenger, in Harrogate, West Yorkshire introduced maximum off-peak fares on all their services in the area. To publicise these, all Harrogate's vehicles gained external stickers proclaiming 'Maximum Off-Peak Fares 9.00 to 16.00 Monday to Saturday Harrogate Area Services', whilst interior notices read 'Welcome Aboard - we're glad to have you travelling with us' and 'Thank you for travelling with us. See you again soon'. In Leeds, the first setting down restrictions which had been applied to all the company's services running out of the city for around fifty years to protect the local municipal operations were at last removed on 28 February, thus allowing local passengers to be carried on 'red' buses. Having gained this concession, West Yorkshire then lost their hospital visitors service (730) from Leeds to Highroyds Hospital, Menston on this same day when the tender was won by Airebus who immediately extended this operation to also serve the Wharfedale General Hospital at Otley. Finally, Harrogate, Otley and Wetherby depots were converted to the Wayfarer ticketing system on the final day of the month, thus continuing the company's progressive updating policy.

More vehicles left the fleet during February when two dual-purpose Leyland Leopards were sold to Norths (dealers) of Sherburn in Elmet and, more surprisingly, two Leyland Nationals departed to join the fleet of London Country North East. Joining the latter within a few days were six Robin Hood-bodied Iveco 49.10 coach-seated minibuses which although ordered by West Yorkshire were never taken into their fleet. Registered E347-52SWY and painted in a livery of red with a black skirt, these vehicles were originally loaned to London Country North East, being purchased by that concern a few months later. By that time, London Country North East, the 71st and last NBC subsidiary to be privatised, plus that company's share in Green Line Travel had come under the control of Alan Stephenson and Parkdale Holdings plc on 22 April, thus giving it distant connections with West Yorkshire Road Car Co. Ltd.

Back in home territory, the non-operational depot at Ilkley which had been 'on the market' for some considerable time was emptied of its stored vehicles by the start of the year and was sold in January to Goldman Investments of Leeds for demolition and eventual development as a shopping area. Meanwhile, at Bradford the projected major revision of the company's services in the Baildon and Shipley area eventually took place on 6 March and included the introduction of six new minibus routes, bringing West Yorkshire's 'little' buses to Bradford for the first time. The services on which they operated surprisingly did not terminate at the Interchange but instead operated from Sunbridge Road on the fringe of the city's shopping area. The vehicles transferred to Bradford depot to join the two which had been used for driver training and route learning purposes since January were the cream & red-liveried Ivecos which had since their delivery in January/February been employed at Harrogate. A further two new examples of this type were added to the Bradford fleet on 1 April and all were given Shipley Hoppa fleet names to publicise the network of

SSF357H, one of Airebus' numerous ex.Lothian Alexander-bodied dual-door Leyland Atlanteans passes through Rawdon on tendered service 830 to Leeds on 17 November 1988.

services on which they were employed. Also added to the fleet were a pair of 16-seat Robin Hood-bodied Iveco 49.10s purchased from East Yorkshire Motor Services. Still wearing their former owner's silver & blue livery, these were given Northern Rose fleet names and were allocated one each to Keighley and Harrogate depots where they were used in a variety of roles including staff transfer buses, driver trainers and for private hire duties.

Further new additions to the fleet in April were nine more Robin Hood-bodied Iveco 49.10 minibuses, six of which were 23-seat buses whilst the remaining three had coach-type seating for 25 passengers. All but one were allocated to Keighley depot, the odd man out going to Otley and all wore the new cream & red Hoppa livery. These and Keighley's other Iveco minibuses were all fitted with a lens in their rear window to assist drivers when reversing. The gradual elimination of NBC's poppy red livery continued with the repainting of vehicles into Tilling red & cream, although there were a number of exceptions such as a couple of the Duple-bodied Leyland Leopards which were repainted all-over white with Northern Rose fleet names and the two York open-top Bristol VRTs which received a new colour scheme of cream with blue bands between decks, blue upper deck front window surrounds and the name 'ViewMaster' on each side between decks. In view of this, it was therefore surprising that when Plaxton-bodied Leyland Leopard 2588 which had been delicenced since 31 July 1987 was returned to service at Keighley depot on 1 March, it still retained its

Two former West Yorkshire Leyland Nationals (1463 & 1442) are seen here on 3 May 1989 in Stevenage bus station in the ownership of Sovereign Bus & Coach Co., another AJS company. 1463 wears the green livery of London Country North East whilst 1442 still carries the red & yellow of its previous owner, BTS of Borehamwood.

NBC poppy red & white dual purpose livery. Even more surprising however was that it had been re-registered AEG984A. Soon afterwards, another dual-purpose Leopard was also given a change of identity when 2555 lost its original registration number UWR771R in favour of AEG917A. At York, Ford Transit minibus 121 was permanently fitted with 'L' plates for use on driver tuition duties but was still available for normal service when required, at which time its 'L' plates were covered over. Also employed on driver tuition and additionally as a staff bus, first at Harrogate depot and later at Bradford, was a coach-seated Iveco 49.10 (D450OKH) which was hired from East Yorkshire from 22 April until the latter part of May.

The last fare boxes in use by the company were replaced on 11 April when Keighley and Grassington depots were converted to Wayfarer electronic ticketing and later that month, several new Hoppa minibus services were introduced in Keighley and those already operating to Thwaites Brow (704) and Fell Lane (706) had hail and ride facilities added to certain sections of their route. Similar facilities were added to Ilkley's town services and the W5 from that town to Otley. On this same date, an entirely new service was inaugurated from Keighley to Guiseley, providing the first ever direct route between these two townships. Numbered 759, the buses scheduled for its operation unusually had special stickers affixed to each side of their bodywork to promote this new service which operated via Bingley, Shipley, Wrose and Greengates whilst in Harrogate, continuing the off-peak maximum fares scheme, all the Hoppa minibuses had banners applied to the top of their windscreens stating '15p Off-Peak Fares 25p', this relating to the child/concessionary rate and the adult fare. Within a few weeks however, as a result of a fares increase, these windscreen banners were modified to read 20p and 30p.

York City & District Carlyle-bodied Ford Transit 121 on driver training duties overtakes Plaxton-bodied Leyland Leopard 2563 opposite York railway station on 1 December 1987. 121 is regarded as a permanent driver tuition vehicle although it is still available for service when required.

Returning to the fleet, a surprise arrival at the end of April was that of an open-top Bristol VRT purchased from East Yorkshire's subsidiary, Scarborough & District. Allocated to Keighley depot, it was acquired for operation on a new tourist service around Bronteland which began on 28 May. Entering service in the cream & poppy red livery in which it arrived, it was in early June repainted into a cream & Tilling red livery similar to that used on the re-seated dual purpose Olympians and incredibly carried Keighley West Yorkshire fleet names despite that company no longer being in existance. Equally surprising, it retained its Scarborough & District fleet number (658) which did not fit into any

An almost empty Plaxton-bodied dual purpose Leyland Leopard 2561 climbs Carr Lane, Wrose on 28 April 1988 on its way to Guiseley on the 759 service. For this duty, it was fitted with a poster on each side which gave details of the route as did a board mounted in its nearside windscreen.

sequence used by West Yorkshire. Also making their debut at around this same time and entering service during May were 16 new Robin Hood-bodied Iveco 49.10 minibuses for York City & District. One was of 25-seat dual purpose configuration whilst the remainder were 19-seat buses and all were painted in a new livery of cream & blue. Another new bus of this same type was added to the West Yorkshire fleet at Harrogate, this being a 23-seater painted in cream & red.

On the reverse side of the coin, three of the Willowbrook 003 dual purpose-bodied Leyland Leopards of York City & District were despatched on loan to West Yorkshire's Leeds

Former Scarborough & District open-top Bristol VRT 658 was acquired by West Yorkshire for use on a tourist service around Bronteland. Repainted into its new owner's cream & red livery and surprisingly given Keighley West Yorkshire fleet names, it is seen here at Haworth railway station on 31 July 1988.

depot from which they operated still with York City fleet names. Nearing the end of their lives with the company, it was perhaps felt extravagant to replace these with West Yorkshire vinyls and in the event all were withdrawn during June and July without returning to York. Leaving the fleet in May were seven surplus dual purpose Leopards which were sold to South Wales Transport for use in their subsidiary

Still painted in NBC-style poppy red & white dual purpose livery, York City & District's Willowbrook 003-bodied Leyland Leopard 2596 poses for the camera in Rougier Street, York on 1 December 1987.

Brewers of Caerau fleet and a Ford Transit minibus which was despatched to London Country North East. Back on the home front, West Yorkshire broke a long-standing tradition of not applying advertising posters to the front of their vehicles when they accepted a contract for the display of posters at each side of the destination box of double deckers (in London Transport fashion) and Keighley Olympian 1822 became the first bus to be so adorned, appearing thus in April.

Above : One of four Bristol VRTs acquired from Alder Valley for use in Keighley, 1947 rests outside the town's bus station on 17 September 1987 between duties on local service 711 to Parkwood Flats.

Right : West Yorkshire finally succumbed to the carrying of advert posters at each side of the front destination screen . Leyland Olympian 1822 became the first bus to be thus adorned and is seen here in Keighley bus station on 8 February 1989 enroute to Skipton on the 666 service from Bradford.

RESTRUCTURING AND DIVISION

Following several months of rumour and speculation, it was announced on 27 May that Parkdale Holdings had sold the prime-positioned bus station at Harrogate to the Ladbroke Group for £2.48million, although the site would continue to be used in its existing role for a short time until it was required by its new owners for redevelopment. This effectively turned the clock back half a century and meant that eventually buses would once again have to terminate in the already-congested streets. Almost before the ink had time to dry on this sale, West Yorkshire announced a massive reorganisation which was to split the company into five smaller units. These comprised three operating companies - York City & District Travel Ltd.; Harrogate & District Travel Ltd. and West Yorkshire Road Car Co. Ltd. - and two non-operational companies, West Yorkshire Engineering and West Yorkshire Management Services. All five companies were to be wholly-owned subsidiaries of West Yorkshire Travel Ltd. which had two directors, Alan Stephenson (Chairman) and Giles Fearnley (Managing Director). Nigel Jolliffe was appointed Managing Director of both York City & District and Harrogate & District while Tom Fox who had previously been Director of Engineering became Managing Director of West Yorkshire Engineering. Stuart Wilde who had held the position of Finance Director since his arrival from East Yorkshire Motor Services in 1987 was appointed Managing Director of West Yorkshire Management Services whilst Andrew Guest who had been Operations Director since the company's privatisation resigned his position and left the company. This left only West Yorkshire Road Car Co. Ltd. without a Managing Director, this post being filled at the beginning of August by Jim Hulme who joined the company from Greater Manchester Buses.

Throughout this period of reorganisation, the company's operations and activities continued in a basically unchanged manner, although during the early summer a new dual-purpose livery was introduced which incorporated white, red, pale blue and black combining the colours used by West Yorkshire, York City and Northern Rose. Several coaches lost their corporate National Express and National Holidays liveries in favour of the company's two-tone blue & white Northern Rose colour scheme and one of the Plaxton Paramount-bodied Leyland Tigers - 2712 - was given National Express names in place of its previous National Holidays identity and had an onboard toilet fitted in preparation for its use on the Newcastle - Chester service. Along with nine other former NBC companies, West

Yorkshire withdrew from National Holidays work and as a result, this livery was quickly eliminated from the fleet, the last vehicle so painted being Leyland Tiger 2403 which was transformed into standard Northern Rose colours at the start of July. Finding themselves with a small surplus of minibuses, West Yorkshire in June despatched four Carlyle-bodied Ford Transits to London Country North East by whom they were put to work in the Hertford area, joining 135 which had travelled south some weeks earlier. All five surprisingly retained their blue Hoppa livery rather than gaining London Country colours. Meanwhile, back in Yorkshire a number of the company's double deckers were fitted with closed circuit television equipment as an anti-vandal and assailant measure. The first to be so treated were Bradford and Keighley depot vehicles, these having one camera fitted to the driver's cab and another on the interior of the front upper deck roof dome.

On 29 May, following increasing traffic congestion in Bradford's city centre, the terminal point of the Shipley Hoppa services was moved from Sunbridge Road to The Tyrls, opposite the Law Courts where a new layby had been constructed. This resulted in a minor revision being made to these routes in order for them to gain access to their new stand. In a new round of service tenders, West Yorkshire lost their 36B route (Leeds - Harewood) to Airebus on 26 June, the latter cutting this back to run only between Leeds and Wigton Moor. Further losses were sustained on 31 July when in York the 27 service from Broadway to York District Hospital was taken over by Reynard Pullman and a week later West Yorkshire cancelled the registration of services 81

Below left : West Yorkshire Carlyle-bodied Ford Transit 125 was one of a number loaned to London Country North East during the summer of 1988. It is seen here, still in blue Hoppa livery leaving Hertford bus station enroute to Bengeo on 20 August 1988.

Below : Ryedale Link Ford Transit F817XUG hurries away from York railway station on its way to Malton via Castle Howard on 2 June 1990.

& 82 which operated between Malton and York. These were replaced by new services between these two points operated by York City & District and by a York - Malton via Sheriff Hutton service maintained by Ryedale Link. Leeds-based Airebus who were still seeking further expansion gained a number of tendered evening and Sunday journeys on the 844 service from Leeds to York and operated these with an unbelievable variety of secondhand vehicles including former Crosville Leyland Leopards and elderly ex. Lothian Regional Transport dual-door Atlanteans.

During the summer of 1988, a small new bus station was opened adjacent to Ilkley railway station and this was immediately used by a number of West Yorkshire's services operating into the town and that of competitor, Pinnacle of Crosshills. Across at Otley, the front of the depot was refurbished to give it an improved appearance and during the course of this work the old corrugated metal front - a remnant of Samuel Ledgard days - was removed.

July witnessed the return of certain properties to the company fold when Alan Stephenson's AJS Group re-purchased the West Yorkshire depots at Leeds, Bradford, Keighley, Otley, Malton, Harrogate and Grassington from Parkdale Holdings. This ensured the continued tenure of these properties for their intended purpose, or so it seemed at the time, but as will be seen from later chapters, changes of policy have a habit of occurring when least expected. In an attempt to attract more passengers, West Yorkshire in July introduced a new travel ticket under the title 'Key Card'. Available for anything from 3 to 13 days travel throughout the company's area, it could be purchased at any West Yorkshire Travel Office or by post from Head Office and its cost ranged from £4 for a child under 14 for 3 days travel to £37 for a family for 13 days. With the introduction of Wayfarer ticket machines at Bradford depot on 21 August, the company's modernisation policy was almost completed and the only vehicles still fitted with the now almost obsolete Almex machines were Bradford depot's Shipley Hoppa minibuses.

Following the departure of the Ford Transit minibuses to London Country North East, another vehicle of this type left its native surrounds in August when it went on loan to Premier Travel at Cambridge. It was soon joined at its new temporary home by two of the Transits from London Country which moved north to Cambridge before the end of that month. The last of the little-used Bristol VRT driver training buses were officially withdrawn on the final day of July and once again the permanent driver tuition fleet was solely maintained by Bristol Lodekkas.

The restructuring of West Yorkshire was completed on 1 September when the new companies all became operational (including York City & District which had become so on 1 March). All were now subsidiaries of the West Yorkshire Travel Group Ltd. which in turn was wholly-owned by WY Group Ltd., a subsidiary of AJS Holdings Ltd. Highlighting these changes, a new leaflet issued by the restructured operating companies showed West Yorkshire's office as being at Vicar Lane Bus Station, Leeds; York City & District at Rougier Street, York and Harrogate & District as being at Harrogate Bus Station, and no mention was made of the company's original headquarters at East Parade, Harrogate. Four days later, on 4 September, all fares in the Harrogate area underwent an increase and coinciding with this, the off-peak fares in that area were reduced in time and extent to become available only from 9.30am to 3.30pm on Mondays to Fridays.

At the start of the new school term, Leeds and Keighley depots both found themselves short of vehicles with which to maintain their school contracts and in an attempt to rectify this situation, six Bristol VRT double deckers were hired from East Yorkshire Motor Services. Four of these were allocated to Leeds depot whilst the remaining two were despatched to Keighley and as a result of none of them being fitted with West Yorkshire's standard ticketing equipment, all were confined to contract duties. Although one returned to its rightful owner on 23 September, the others remained at Leeds and Keighley until mid-late October with the last returning to Hull on the 26th of that month. The seven remaining withdrawn Leyland Nationals were sold to Martins (dealers) of Middlewich on 20 September and a month later, thirteen dual-purpose Leyland Leopards were disposed of to dealer Stuart Johnson and three Ford Transit minibuses to Carlyle, Birmingham. Prior to this, as a result of London Country North East losing their contracted minibus services in the Hertford area to Jubilee Coaches of Stevenage, the

Ford Transits which had been on loan to London Country since May/June were returned to West Yorkshire. Only one of these (135) re-entered service in its native Yorkshire however, this being allocated to Wetherby depot on 1 November. Perhaps more surprising however was the return to service of Leyland National 1478 which, after a long period in store still wearing its Metrobus Verona green & buttermilk livery was re-instated at York early in November repainted into a cream livery with blue relief but bearing no fleet names or numbers.

The service network continued to undergo constant revision in order to meet new demands and on 5 September limited stop conditions were imposed between Keighley and Five Lane Ends on the 759 service from Keighley to Guiseley, this section of the route already being covered by other conventional West Yorkshire stopping services. On that same day Pinnacle Coaches of Crosshills inaugurated two new competitive services from Keighley, one running to Skipton, the other to Cowling whilst on 15 September the peak-hours limited stop X67 service from Bradford to Keighley was extended to Silsden. A new Mondays only operation was introduced on 12 September from Wetherby to Selby with one journey in each direction and on 26 September the licences for all York's city services were transferred from West Yorkshire Road Car Co. Ltd. to York City & District who also became joint operators of several of the services running to places outside the city.

Having restructured the former West Yorkshire empire into several smaller companies, it was decided in October to reorganise Northern Rose, the company's private hire and coaching arm. This resulted in most of Northern Rose's operations being concentrated at Keighley from the end of that month and West Yorkshire's National Express work being shared between Leeds and Bradford depots. York was to retain only its National Express Rapide duties whilst Harrogate, for many years the hub of the company's

coaching operations, was to cease running private hire, excursions and minibreak holidays. Following closely on the heels of the above came the news that all Harrogate depot's vehicle maintenance at Grove Park depot was to cease and would in future be undertaken in the chassis shop at the West Yorkshire Engineering workshops in the town. Coinciding with this move were several management changes and the relinquishing of the post of Group Managing Director by Giles Fearnley who moved to AJS Holdings following that company's reorganisation to become Group Services Director with special responsibility for support services. These included Parkdale Pension Company, recently purchased from Parkdale Holdings plc and renamed AJS Pensions Management Ltd. The position of Group Managing Director was not to be filled in view of the recent company restructuring and West Yorkshire Travel was now renamed WY Group Ltd. With the continual changes which were being made within the former West Yorkshire empire, one could not help but wonder what would come next, especially when a 'For Sale' notice appeared outside the Head Office building in East Parade, Harrogate !

In the meantime, a new travel scheme was introduced in the Harrogate area on 17 October which offered cheap travel to senior citizens resident in that town and Knaresborough. Under the title 'Senior Citizens Saver Club', with a super saver card discount fares were available between 9.30am and 3.00pm on all local services in Harrogate and Knaresborough with a maximum of 20p. Special low fares were also available on certain journeys between Harrogate and Leeds, Bradford, Ripon and York and special trips were to be organised for Club members from time to time, these being publicised in a free newsletter. Whilst senior citizens in the Harrogate area were being offered these travel incentives, those in York faced increasing costs when York City & District put up the price of pensioners bus passes from £24 to £26 per year and rose the maximum fare from 20p to 25p.

A new round of tendering in West Yorkshire saw the company lose the W5 minibus service from Otley to Ilkley and certain journeys on the X3/X30 Otley to Leeds route to Rhodes Coaches of Yeadon and the 830/1 Leeds - Otley routes to Airebus from 30 October. Airebus also gained the Bradford - Leeds/Bradford Airport - Otley X1 service from Rhodes Coaches on that same date whilst West Yorkshire introduced a new local circular minibus service in Aireborough numbered A1, operating this from Otley depot.

During the early part of November, one of West Yorkshire's surplus Ford Transit minibuses (124) was despatched on loan to East Yorkshire Motor Services whilst in the following month one of York City & District's Transits was repainted into that company's new cream & blue livery, heralding the gradual transformation of the fleet into this colour scheme. Keighley's open-top Bristol VRT which, since the withdrawal of the Bronteland tourist service on which it had been employed during the summer had seen little use except for occasional driver training purposes, was used as a 'Santa' bus by the Co-operative stores in Harrogate, Knaresborough

Top left : One of the full-height ECW-bodied Bristol VRTs hired from East Yorkshire Motor Services, 981 still retained its rightful owner's destnation blinds which on this occasion showed a Hull area service, the 153 to Ferriby.

Left : One of the oldest coaches to sport the attractive two-tone blue & white livery of Northern Rose was 2556, a Plaxton-bodied Leopard seen here about to enter Hammerton Street depot, Bradford on 30 July 1988.

and Wetherby during the final days of November. Following these duties it was decorated with fairy lights and, playing Christmas Carols, was used in Keighley to mark the start of the festive season. For the first time for many years, West Yorkshire Road Car Co. Ltd. operated services on Christmas Day, these being financially supported by Metro. Only Leeds and Keighley depots were involved however (the services operated being the 655, 660/1, 663, 670, 733, 741, 784 and 798) and the solitary bus needed for the 660/1 Bradford - Baildon services, although operated by a Bradford driver was provided by Keighley depot to save Hammerton Street depot at Bradford having to be opened.

The final day of 1989 saw West Yorkshire begin a new service - numbered 805 from Keighley to Horton in Ribblesdale which incorporated a number of short workings between Settle and Horton. Running on Saturdays only and operated by a Keighley depot minibus, this replaced a service previously maintained by Whaites of Settle and in addition to providing much needed transport for those resident in that part of the Yorkshire Dales, it was believed that it would also appeal to those who enjoyed hiking and country persuits.

Thus another year ended - a year in which wide ranging changes had been made to the company's structure, completely altering its face and operations. One wondered what 1989 would bring, and what further reorganisation would take place, and indeed how successful some of the new smaller units would be in the face of increasing competition from hungry independents. The company's old-established Head Office in East Parade, Harrogate had closed before Christmas and its remaining functions were now performed at several temporary locations within the company's other properties until new headquarters could be found. Yes, yet another era had drawn to a close. . . .

1989 began with Harrogate & District suffering the loss of some of their tendered services which, on 3 January were taken over by Reynard Pullman from their local base at Manse Lane, Knaresborough. Pullman's main operation was on the Harrogate local service to Hornbeam Park via Pannal although they also gained some journeys to Kingsley Drive

and Penny Pot as well as reaching Otley on the 775 service and all were worked with conventional size single deckers. West Yorkshire inaugurated but one new service during this, the first month of the year, that being the minibus-operated W7 from Otley to Middleton Hospital on the fringe of Ilkley which had but one journey in each direction each day. On 13 January, the night service 939 from Bradford to Baildon had one journey extended to Guiseley and continued to run on Friday and Saturday nights only whilst three days later, the X30 from Otley to Leeds which had been operated jointly with Rhodes Coaches was converted into a conventional stopping service, renumbered 732 and passed solely to Rhodes' control.

West Yorkshire's oldest Leyland National, 1411 which was the first bus to be painted into the company's new Tilling red & cream livery and had been retained in semi-preservation long after all its sisters had departed, was finally withdrawn on the last day of 1988 and offered for sale. Leaving the fleet in January, it was joined by 9 dual-purpose Leopards, 1 Plaxton Paramount-bodied Tiger coach, 2 Ford Transit minibuses and 5 Bristol VRTs. Of these, three of the Leopards passed to London Country North East and the two Transits (including 128 which was already on loan) went to East Yorkshire , the Tiger coach to Yorkshire Traction and a Leopard - albeit accident damaged but repairable - to Dodsworths of Boroughbridge. The remainder were sold to dealers. On the home front, three of the Plaxton Paramount 3200-bodied Tiger coaches were downgraded to dual purpose status and fitted with ticketing equipment whilst somewhat surprisingly, a former United Counties Plaxton-bodied Bristol RELH coach was hired from the Northern Bus Co., North Anston, Sheffield for two days in mid-January for National Express duties.

Now that West Yorkshire's central repair workshops were a separate subsidiary (WY Engineering Ltd.), outside work was being actively solicited and brought a contract from the Ministry of Defence for the repainting of a number of their Wadham Stringer-bodied Dodge vehicles. Having now vacated Head Office and placed this on the market for sale, Parkdale Holdings now embarked upon an asset realisation

programme which during the months ahead was to witness the disposal of numerous West Yorkshire properties. Unfortunately for Parkdale however, Leeds City planners rejected an outline application to build shops on the site presently occupied by Wetherby depot and bus station, thus preventing its immediate sale. Following the disposal of the company's former Head Office in East Parade to Harrogate District Council, part of the central repair works complex at Harrogate was sold for redevelopment, this comprising the chassis shop in Myrtle Road which was to be demolished, and the nearby Westmoreland House. This resulted in the functions carried out by the chassis shop being transferred to the already overcrowded body shop which was now far too small to cope with the size of the fleet. The bus station at Otley was also sold for redevelopment into a new shopping area which, when completed would incorporate a tiny new bus station, and the old site was progressively closed between the latter part of 1988 and the spring of 1989 to allow building work to take place. The AJS Group also began to look at their own property portfolio and began a programme of disposals by placing Grove Park depot at Harrogate on the market. Finally, after surviving in several temporary locations since the vacation of East Parade, Harrogate at the end of 1988, West Yorkshire Road Car Co. Ltd. moved into its new Head Office at 4 Sheepscar Court, Meanwood Road, Leeds early in March.

In comparison with the past, February and March proved to be comparatively quiet months as far as the fleet and operations were concerned. One of the MCW Metroliner double deck coaches together three Plaxton Paramount-bodied Leyland Tigers - including the one purchased from Yorkshire Traction in 1983 - were sold to that company on 6 February, whilst joining the fleet on 15 March was a Leyland National hired from Scarborough & District which was at first

allocated to Leeds depot. An acute shortage of vehicles at Bradford early in March caused several journeys to be lost and in a bid to overcome this situation, several duties had to be temporarily covered by Keighley depot. So desparate did this shortage become, that Bradford had on more than one occasion to resort to using one of their highfloor Plaxton Paramount 3500-bodied Leyland Tiger coaches on stage carriage duties and in addition use minibuses on conventional bus routes. A start was made on the repainting of the company's blue-liveried Iveco minibuses into the cream & red colour scheme whilst at York the Ford Transits continued to be transformed by their receipt of York City & District's cream & blue livery. Plaxton Paramount-bodied

Above : Carlyle-bodied Ford Transit 120 looks extremely smart in its new York City & District cream & blue livery as it passes the city's railway station in March 1989 on its way to Beckfield Lane on city service 21. (J. Whitmore)

Left : One of the Leyland Nationals hired from Scarborough & District, 132 hurries through Rawdon on its way to Bradford on the limited stop X1 service on 28 April 1989. Although retaining its owner's fleet names and advertising posters, it was fitted with a West Yorkshire destination blind.

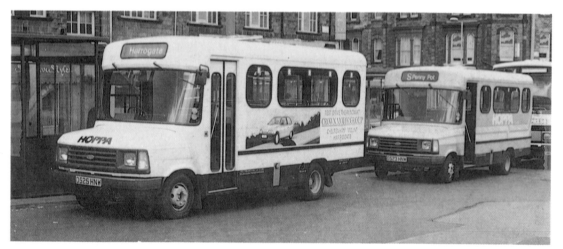

Above : Carlyle-bodied Ford Transit 115 in all over advertising for Crown Motor Group stands with normal-liveried 108 in Harrogate bus station in September 1987.

Right : 2613, an ECW-bodied Leyland Leopard in National Holidays livery rests on the forecourt of Grove Park depot, Harrogate after working a stage carriage duty on the 36 route from Leeds.

HARROGATE
& DISTRICT

Leyland Tiger 2704 appeared in March in a new cream & red livery derived from that applied to the re-seated Leyland Olympians to reflect its new status as a dual-purpose vehicle. Given new-style fleet names its appearance was both striking and attractive. On the deficit side, the only other vehicles to be withdrawn for disposal during February/March were the former East Yorkshire coach-seated Iveco 91, which still retained its original owner's colours and Leyland National 1509 which was severely damaged in an accident between Utley and Steeton on 21 February.

Although Harrogate & District had been operational for several months, it was not until mid-March that the vehicles of this fleet began to receive their new owner's fleet names and legal lettering, the latter now showing the registered address as being at Barleycorn Yard, Walmgate, York which was the same as that of York City & District.

In complete contrast to the two previous months, April proved to be one of great activity with expansion in one direction and contraction in another. Looking first at the service changes which took place that month, West Yorkshire regained some of its previous operations following the sudden demise of Airebus following prohibition notices being served on them by the Traffic Commissioners. This brought the tendered operations between Leeds and York back into the company's fold on 9 April and three days later restored the X1, 830 and 831 services to West Yorkshire operation. The unexpected sudden acquisition of these operations created a shortage of vehicles with which to operate them and led to the hiring of a second Leyland National and a dual-purpose Plaxton-bodied Leyland Leopard from Scarborough & District from 13 April. Also on this date, a pair of East Lancs-bodied Leyland Atlanteans

Plaxton Paramount-bodied Leyland Tiger 2704 wears the new red & cream dual purpose livery and fleet name applied in 1989 as it rests outside Vicar Lane bus station, Leeds on 25 may 1989 after operating the 734 service from Ilkley.

Hired Hyndburn Transport East Lancs-bodied Leyland Atlantean 183 stands alongside West Yorkshire's Duple-bodied Leyland Leopard 2604 in Vicar Lane bus station, Leeds on 26 April 1989.

HARROGATE
& DISTRICT

Harrogate & District Leyland Lynx 1207 was a mere two months old when photographed in Harrogate bus station on 4 June 1989. In April 1990, this bus together with its five sisters was transferred to York City & District for use on city services.

were hired from Hyndburn Transport for use at Leeds depot on contract duties. One of these proved troublesome from the start however and was exchanged for another bus of the same type after a few days. A third Hyndburn Atlantean arrived at the end of April and together with its two sisters was occasionally to be found on normal stage carriage services from Leeds depot in addition to being employed on schools contracts. Harrogate & District received six new Leyland Lynx single deckers which differed from the original pair of this model by being fitted with Cummins engines instead of Gardner power units and these quickly settled down on the prestigious Leeds - Harrogate - Ripon service which was operated jointly with United. Another stranger to the company was a Reeve Burgess Beaver-bodied Iveco minibus which was borrowed from its manufacturer for evaluation purposes for a few days at the end of April. This was used at Keighley depot on driver training duties and was not placed in revenue-earning service during its brief stay.

Leaving the group on the penultimate day of April were another five coaches, these all being Plaxton-bodied Leyland Tigers which were sold to National Express' new subsidiary, Dorset Travel Services of Wareham. In addition, the two ex.East Yorkshire Iveco minicoaches left the Northern Rose fleet to join London Country North East, but more surprisingly, the WY Travel Group announced in April that it was to withdraw completely from National Express and coaching activities and that the remaining coaches were to be sold to a newly-formed company set up by National Express under the title of Yorkshire Voyager. Although no date was set for the commencement of this new operation, it was anticipated that it would be towards the end of June. Following much speculation as to the future of what remained of the group's central repair works at Harrogate it was confirmed that WY Engineering Ltd. would continue to lease the bodyshop from Parkdale but that the workforce was to be cut by 50% to a mere 50 employees. Meanwhile, WY Management Services had left their offices in East Parade and had moved to Regent Parade, Harrogate next door to the Head Office of AJS Holdings Ltd.

Opposite page.

Left column, top to bottom :

Still wearing its Yorkshire Coastliner livery, dual purpose Leyland Olympian 5519 is seen here in Eastgate, Leeds on Yorkshire Rider's cross-city stage carriage service 42 to Old Farnley on 19 May 1990.

A former Reeve Burgess demonstrator and still sporting its demonstration livery, Iveco minibus G449LKW is seen in Harrogate bus station on 22 May 1990 after being purchased by Harrogate Independent Travel (Challenger).

Keighley & District Leyland Olympian 363 in its new unimpressive chinchilla & red livery leaves Bradford Interchange on 26 April 1990 at the start of its journey to Oakworth on service 665. Unlike some repaints, it did not have a narrow blue band below its upper deck windows.

Keighley & District's oldest Leyland Leopard, a Plaxton-bodied example of 1979 vintage, 221 is seen arriving in Keighley from Airedale Hospital during its final week in service on 1 June 1990.

Right column, top to bottom :

Transferred from Yorkshire Rider to West Yorkshire, Plaxton-bodied Leyland Leopard 1529 was repainted into an all-over cream livery and allocated to Hammerton Street depot, Bradford. It is seen here in Bradford's Interchange on 8 October 1989.

Operating an Otley town service on 30 March 1990, Carlyle-bodied Ford Transit 1743 still carried its West Yorkshire blue Hoppa livery but had gained a dark red legal lettering vinyl giving the registered address as Yorkshire Rider's headquarters in Leeds.

Still wearing its white, blue, red & black Northern Rose livery embellished with Keighley & District fleet name vinyls, Duple-bodied Leyland Leopard 2605 rests in Keighley bus station following a schools contract duty on 11 October 1989.

Harrogate Independent Travel D924KWW, an NCME-bodied Dodge S46 minibus passes Harrogate bus station enroute to Knaresborough in May 1990.

EXPANSION AND CONTRACTION

Seeking to eliminate the competition to Harrogate & District in their home town, AJS Holdings in April gained a controlling interest in Harrogate Independent Travel, a company set up in 1987 by a co-operative of former West Yorkshire employees to operate services in Harrogate and Knaresborough. Starting with a fleet of six leased NCME-bodied Dodge minibuses and operating under the title of 'Challenger', this independent had more than doubled its fleet since its formation and now had 14 vehicles including a former London Transport DMS-type Daimler Fleetline double decker and some full-sized coaches. Under AJS control, it was intended that Challenger would continue to operate autonomously and would not be integrated into the Harrogate & District undertaking.

Above : Harrogate Independent Travel Wadham Stringer-bodied Leyland Swift E963NMK picks up its Harrogate-bound passengers in a narrow street near Knaresborough bus station.

Left : Harrogate Independent Travel (Challenger) used stops in Station Parade, Harrogate, outside the bus station. One of their NCME-bodied Dodge S46s - D924KWW - is seen at this point awaiting its Ripon-bound passengers.

HARROGATE
INDEPENDENT
TRAVEL

Following a month of great activity, May proved to be the complete opposite with few changes taking place within the fleet or its operations. During the second part of the month the Hoppa and conventional routes serving the Baildon and Shipley areas underwent revision to provide a better local network whilst the 830 route from Leeds to Otley was withdrawn completely and its sister, the 831 passed to Rhodes Coaches of Yeadon. The accident damaged Leyland National 1509, found to be beyond economic repair, was sold for scrap and the three hired Hyndburn Atlanteans all returned home in mid-May and were immediately put up for sale on their arrival back in Accrington.

Despite beliefs that the restructuring of West Yorkshire had been completed some months earlier, at the end of May WY Engineering was renamed Premier Engineering Ltd. although its functions remained unchanged. Almost immediately following this change of name, it was announced that Keighley and Grassington depots were to be separated from West Yorkshire Road Car Co. Ltd. and placed under the

control of yet another newly-created company, Keighley & District Travel Ltd. Although no date was given for the launching of this new WY Group subsidiary, it was expected that it would become operational within a couple of months.

During the early part of June, two vehicles were obtained on loan from their makers for evaluation purposes, one being an Optare Delta--bodied DAF, the other a 37-seat Reeve Burgess-bodied Leyland Swift. The DAF-Delta arrived in all-white livery and was used for a week by Keighley depot on both local and out of town services whilst the Leyland Swift after being examined by Harrogate & District passed to Harrogate Independent Travel and thence to York City & District before returning to its owners on 19 June. Although during this time the two Leyland Nationals and the dual purpose Leopard hired from Scarborough & District were still

Having served longer in all-over advertising liveries than any other West Yorkshire vehicle, Leyland National 1515 is seen here on 20 April 1989 in Keighley bus station carrying its final livery for Northern Rose, the company's coaching arm.

hard at work, the Leopard left Bradford depot to return home during the final week of June. The only other vehicle which should perhaps be mentioned at this point is Leyland National 1515 which, after carrying all-over advertising liveries since August 1983 - latterly for Northern Rose - was restored to fleet colours in mid-June.

On the fourth day of June, the hail and ride facilities on Keighley local services 706 and 707 to Fell Lane were withdrawn, restoring these routes to conventional operation while on the final day of that month applications were made to the Traffic Commissioners for new operators licences for Harrogate & District, Keighley & District and West Yorkshire Road Car Co. Ltd., the number of discs for each being 65, 120 and 140 respectively. The news of the month was however, most unexpectedly, that Pateley Bridge depot was to be offered for sale by auction on 27 June with vacant possession from 30 June. The site comprised the depot, bus station, sales kiosk, wooden shop and the adjacent field and had outline planning permission for the building of 25 residential units. Quickly sold for £405,000, it was some months however before the site was cleared in preparation for the new development and eventually the prefabricated depot structure was dismantled in October after being sold to Motley of Glazefield, Pateley Bridge for the housing of his two buses.

July dawned and with it came the end of yet another era when on the first day of the month the company's travel office attached to Otley depot was closed. Just less than four weeks later, the bus station at Knaresborough was also closed and vacated, resulting in the vehicles serving this already heavily-congested market town having to pick up and set down their passengers in Fisher Street and Chapel Street much to the displeasure of Harrogate District Council.

Soon after the return of the hired Leyland Leopard to its owners, Scarborough & District, another Leyland National was received from that operator, this making its debut at Keighley depot on 9 July. Its stay was to be comparatively brief however and by the end of the month it, along with its two sisters, were returned to Scarborough from whence they had come. Depleting the fleet further, albeit only temporarily, was the unexpected departure of Duple-bodied Leyland Leopard 2606 which in the early hours of 18 July was stolen from Keighley bus station. Despite every effort being made by the Police to trace its whereabouts, it was not until six days later that it was eventually found, some 200 miles away north of the border, in Ayr. With great relief that it was still basically in the same condition in which it departed, a driver was despatched to Scotland for its collection but, obviously not wishing to be reunited with its colleagues at Keighley too quickly, 2606 broke down at Settle on its way back to Yorkshire and completed its journey behind Keighley depot's towing wagon !

In an attempt to obtain a more accurate mileage recording, all the group's vehicles were equipped with Engler Hubodometers which were fitted to the offside rear hub. This enabled the Group to monitor their fleet with greater accuracy than had previously been possible and proved beneficial in terms of both fuel and maintenance costings.

A Stemco Engler Hubodometer as used on AJS Group vehicles.

Above right : One of the National Express Rapide-liveried Plaxton Paramount 3500-bodied Leyland Tigers sold to Yorkshire Voyager upon its formation, 2410 awaits collection by its new owner behind Hammerton Street depot, Bradford on 15 September 1989.

Right : Also sold to Yorkshire Voyager was 2003, a Plaxton Paramount 4000-bodied Neoplan which, having had its Northern Rose fleet names removed, stands on the ramp to Hammerton Street depot, Bradford from where it was temporarily operated by its new owner in September 1989.

Having had its Northern Rose fleet names removed in preparation for its sale to Yorkshire Voyager, MCW Metroliner Rapide coach 2005 stands temporarily unused behind Hammerton Street depot, Bradford.

Although it had been expected that West Yorkshire would by now have completed their withdrawal from National Express operations, delays in the setting up by National Express of their new Yorkshire Voyager Travel Services subsidiary resulted in the company continuing to maintain their contracted services during the first weeks of July and it was not until the 25th. of that month that they were finally able to rid themselves of these duties. Despite their intention to use the former Airebus depot at Evanston Avenue, Leeds, negotiations for these premises had not been completed when Yorkshire Voyager eventually became operational and as a short--term measure, only 4 of the 23 vehicles acquired

Still in blue Hoppa livery, Robin Hood-bodied Iveco minibus 152 is seen here in Keighley bus station on 20 April 1989 whilst being used for driver training purposes.

Opposite page.

Left column, top to bottom :

Seen after the acquisition of West Yorkshire by Yorkshire Rider, Bristol VRT 745 leaves Vicar Lane bus station, Leeds on a 734 journey to Ilkley on 13 January 1990. Still sporting its West Yorkshire fleet name and livery, it also carries a side poster for that company.

One of Keighley & District's vehicles to be given an experimental livery towards the end of June 1990 was Leyland Olympian 354 which had its window frames painted red and had a thin blue line added above its red skirt. Seen here in Keighley depot on 25 June 1990 it had been used on a private hire duty.

Former West Yorkshire Duple dual purpose-bodied Leyland Leopard 1552 with Yorkshire Rider vinyls covering its original owner's names leaves Beadford Interchange at the start of its journey to Otley in April 1990. It was unusually painted in Tilling red & white livery (rather than cream) and had black window frames and skirt.

Despite sporting Yorkshire Rider Huddersfield fleet names, ex.West Yorkshire Leyland National 1344 was still working for Bradford depot early in April 1990 when it was caught by the camera arriving at Bradford Interchange from Otley on route 654.

Right column, top to bottom :

Having lost its cream & red Shipley Hoppa colours in favour of Yorkshire Rider's standard Micro Rider livery, former West Yorkshire Robin Hood-bodied Iveco 2079 stands at the Wibsey terminus of route 845 in May 1990.

Harrogate & District Robin Hood-bodied Iveco 138 passes the town's bus station in the autumn of 1989 enroute to Crossways on a local service. Originally delivered in blue Hoppa livery, it later gained its owner's new standard cream & red colours.

Amongst the first former West Yorkshire vehicles to receive standard Yorkshire Rider livery was Bristol VRT 725 which was also given Yorkshire Rider Leeds fleet names. It is seen here resting in Vicar Lane bus station, Leeds on 30 March 1990.

Looking immaculate is freshly repainted York City & District Bristol VRT 1767, pictured here in Vicar Lane bus station Leeds whilst working a duty to Wetherby on the 799 service on 25 May 1989.

from West Yorkshire were at first put to use by the new company. These were operated two each from Bradford and Keighley depots on the Rapide 561 service to London and the remaining coaches were temporarily placed in store at West Yorkshire depots. The four coaches concerned continued to operated on West Yorkshire discs for a few weeks until licences were granted to Voyager and, as a further temporary measure, servicing facilities were provided at West Yorkshire's Hammerton Street depot, Bradford.

Prior to the above happenings however, it was revealed on 18 July that AJS Holdings Ltd. had sold West Yorkshire Road Car Co. Ltd. to Rider Holdings for £3.5million and that the transfer of ownership would take place at midnight on 12 August. The deal included 123 vehicles and most services operated from Leeds, Bradford and Otley depots. The depots themselves were not part of the package however and remained in the ownership of AJS Holdings, although the lease on these would be transferred to Yorkshire Rider for a limited period of time. Rider Holdings itself was a comparatively new company, having been formed on 21 October 1988 under an Employee Share Ownership Plan to acquire the former West Yorkshire PTE company, Yorkshire Rider Ltd. Thus, despite firm resistance during the 'seventies to take-over approaches by the then West Yorkshire PTE and the refusal by the Department of Transport to allow the West Yorkshire PTA to bid for the company upon its sale by the NBC, West Yorkshire Road Car Co. Ltd. had finally capitulated and effectively reached the end of the road. The news that the company was to be fully integrated into Yorkshire Rider after a period of 3 - 6 months was met with great sadness and it quickly became obvious that it would not be long before the smart Tilling red & cream livery and old-established West Yorkshire fleet name would become no more than memories. Having to date only applied the new Harrogate & District fleet name to a handful of vehicles, a start was made in July on affixing new vinyl fleet names and legal lettering to the whole of the Harrogate fleet, this task being completed during the early part of August. Similarly, in preparation for the transfer of West Yorkshire to its new owners, the former company's fleet name was eliminated from the Keighley-based fleet during the first couple of weeks in August when Keighley & District legal lettering and temporary fleet name vinyls were applied to all that depot's vehicles and those outstationed at Grassington.

Receiving attention to its batteries in Roseville Road depot, Leeds on 25 May 1989 is short Leyland National 1021 which carried extensive advertising for the free service to Safeway Supermarket upon which it was usually employed. Being unable to carry its fleet name in the customary position on the cove panels, this was repositioned below the driver's side window.

Almost unbelievably, the AJS-owned companies underwent yet another series of name changes at this same time when the WY Group Ltd. who owned Keighley & District, Harrogate & District, York City & District and the investment in Harrogate Independent Travel was renamed the North of England Travel Group Ltd. Coinciding with this, AJS Holdings Ltd. became the AJS Group Ltd. and was split into two parts, one heading up the bus operations, the other - AJS Services Ltd - taking control of the Pensions Management company, an Executive Recruitment company and Premier Engineering (Harrogate) Ltd. WY Management Services Ltd. was also a subsidiary of the North of England Travel Group Ltd. whilst ABC Parts Ltd. which provided a function for both the WY Group and the EYMS Group was a wholly-owned subsidiary of AJS Services Ltd. During this reorganisation, Tom Fox, the Managing Director of Premier Engineering relinquished his position and left the Group.

With the pending departure of West Yorkshire from the North of England Travel Group, the licences for all that company's services were cancelled on 21 July and replaced by new licences issued to the separate operating companies. Although the majority of the licences concerned had been held by West Yorkshire at Sheepscar Court, Leeds, those now re-issued to Harrogate & District had previously been in the name of West Yorkshire Road Car Co. Ltd. at PO Box 24, East Parade, Harrogate. Those now granted to Keighley & District showed their registered address as being at Sheepscar Court, Leeds and surprisingly included Ilkley local services W1, W4 and W7 plus the Bradford - Keighley 689, all of which were scheduled to pass to Rider Holdings on 12 August. Obviously an oversight when these new applications were made, the licences for these services were cancelled on 6 August. A further twist to this saga related to the Dales services 71, 76, 272, 800 and 809 and Skipton town service

Former West Yorkshire Leyland National 1422 following its withdrawal from service gained a new lease of life when it was purchased by Scottish independent, Morrow of Clydebank. Repainted into its new owner's colours, it picks up a solitary passenger at the Old Kilpatrick terminus of route 86 in February 1989.

A long way from home, Northern Rose-liveried Plaxton Paramount 3500-bodied Leyland Tiger 2412 is seen here at The Village Inn, Swanwick on 10 May 1988 whilst operating one of the company's extended tours to Dorset.

Plaxton-bodied Leyland Leopard dual purpose 2586 shows off its new Keighley & District fleet names as it leaves Keighley bus station enroute to Airedale Hospital on 11 October 1989.

Having lost its original blue Hoppa livery in favour of Harrogate & District's cream & red colours, 160, a former Southdown Robin Hood-bodied Iveco traverses Park Row, Knaresborough on its way to Harrogate on route 57 on 21 June 1989.

Painted in an all-white livery, Plaxton Paramount-bodied Leyland Tiger 2701 had its Northern Rose fleet names covered by Keighley & District vinyls when it was downgraded to dual purpose status. Pictured in Keighley bus station on 11 October 1989, it was working the never well patronised 759 service to Guiseley.

Dual purpose-seated Leyland Olympian 1831 which began life as a standard stage carriage vehicle had gained Keighley & District fleet names to its predominantly cream livery by the time it was photographed in Keighley bus station in September 1989.

Despite still carrying Yorkshire Coastliner's white and two-tone blue livery, ex.Alder Valley Bristol VRT 1700 was given Keighley & District fleet name vinyls when this new company was formed. It is seen here resting in Keighley bus station between duties on town service 711 to Parkwood Flats on 11 October 1989.

Parked at the front of Grove Park depot, Harrogate on 22 November 1989 is Plaxton-bodied Leyland Leopard 2571, which as its transfers indicate was part of the Harrogate & District fleet.

ECW-bodied Leyland Olympian 1827 turns from Bridge Street, Bradford into the Interchange at the end of its journey from Skipton on 15 September 1989. Sporting Keighley & District fleet names, it has had its original opening-type upper deck bulkhead windows replaced by fixed glazing.

Despite still wearing Northern Rose livery, Plaxton Paramount-bodied Leyland Tiger 2705 had its rear fleet name replaced by a Keighley & District vinyl and its boot lid was altered to show a Keighley telephone number. It is seen here in company with sister vehicle 2710 outside Keighley bus station on 11 October 1989.

73, the licences for which were issued to Keighley & District Travel Ltd. t/a Craven Bus at Sheepscar Court. The Craven Bus name had not at that time appeared on any of the company's vehicles or on publicity material and indeed has not done subsequently. Although new vinyls showing West Yorkshire Road Car Co's Sheepscar Court, Leeds legal address had been produced, these had never been applied to any of the company's vehicles which all continued to show PO Box 24, East Parade, Harrogate on their legal panel and continued to do so to the end of West Yorkshire's operations on 12 August.

Still seeking expansion whenever the opportunity arose, Reynard Pullman of York registered three Monday to Friday and two Saturday journeys on the 844 service from York to Leeds from 31 July and in addition registered one solitary journey Monday to Friday on York local service 7A from Heslington Hall to the city centre.

As the day of West Yorkshire's demise drew nearer, the company's name was removed from all its premises in Harrogate, Keighley, Wetherby and Malton leaving only those in Bradford, Leeds and Otley thus adorned and it was wondered just how long these would survive unscathed. Saturday 12 August came all too soon and on the final day of operation much activity took place between Keighley and the depots which were to be taken over by Yorkshire Rider, repositioning vehicles to ensure that those not involved in the sale were at Keighley before midnight. To mark the end of the company in Bradford, Hammerton Street depot returned

through time by crew-operating the final journey from Bradford Interchange to Baildon and back, with the conductor wearing an old-style uniform and issuing tickets from a vintage Bellgraphic machine. Showing pre-PTE service number 61 on its destination screen instead of the current 661, a Tilling red & cream Bristol VRT (1765) was selected for this journey which was to be the last operated by the company to return to the Interchange.

Above right : York City & District Bristol VRT 1742 was one of a number of that company's vehicles to carry an all-over advertising livery. Passing York railway station on 1 December 1987, it is enroute to Wetherby on service 79.

Right : Having arrived from Otley on the 654 service on the final night of West Yorkshire operation before the company's passege to Yorkshire Rider, all-white liveried Duple dual purpose-bodied Leyland Leopard 2601 prepares to leave for Hammerton Street depot a few minutes before midnight. Behind it is sister vehicle 2602 in standard red & cream livery.

The last duty performed by a West Yorkshire vehicle at Bradford prior to the take-over of that company by Yorkshire Rider was that from Baildon to Bradford on the 661 service on 12 August 1989. This was performed by Bristol VRT 1765 which is seen here after its final arrival in Bradford's Interchange shortly before midnight. Note the destination indicator showed the service number as 61 rather than the PTE-style 661.

RIDER GAINS CONTROL

Thus an era had ended and West Yorkshire was no more - or was it ? During the night of 12/13 August, new legal ownership vinyls were applied to all the vehicles acquired by Yorkshire Rider, these showing that the company was still named West Yorkshire Road Car Co. Ltd. but that the registered address had now become 1 Swinegate, Leeds, the headquarters of Yorkshire Rider. The fleet name and livery carried by all the acquired vehicles remained unchanged , somehow giving them a false sense of security, and on Sunday 13 August operations continued in much the same way they had done on previous Sundays. Several routes radiating from Leeds to such places as Wetherby, Harrogate, Ripon and York and from Bradford to Keighley and Skipton which had previously been jointly operated between various companies within the Group were not included in the deal and thus passed completely to the Keighley, Harrogate or York companies whilst Keighley & District relinquished their share of the 784 and X84 services from Skipton to Leeds to Yorkshire Rider.

As a result of the sudden deterioration to the road surface on a section between Haworth and Stanbury which had led to at least three buses being involved in accidents, the services from Bradford were suspended at Haworth during the last week in August and replaced by a Hoppa minibus which then travelled to Stanbury via a narrow moorland road in order to avoid the offending stretch. This continued until the remedial work by the Council was completed and it was not until mid-September that normal operations could be resumed.

Just as it was appearing that little had changed since that fateful day in August, Yorkshire Rider transferred two of their Plaxton Derwent-bodied Leyland Leopards from their Calderdale division to West Yorkshire at Bradford and, after surprisingly being repainted into Tilling red & cream livery and having West Yorkshire fleet names applied, these two dual purpose-seated single deckers took up their new duties from Hammerton Street depot on 25 August. The last vehicles to retain Almex ticket machines - Bradford depot's Shipley Hoppa minibuses - were fitted with Wayfarer equipment by the beginning of September, bringing them into line with West Yorkshire and Yorkshire Rider's standard fares collection system and the faithful Almex was now extinct.

The need for additional vehicles led to the loan of Yorkshire Rider Freight Rover Sherpa minibus 1765 to Otley

The legal lettering panel before and after the acquisition of West Yorkshire Road Car Co. Ltd. by Yorkshire Rider. Although they were produced, the vinyls showing the company's Sheepscar Court head office address were never applied to any vehicles.

YORKSHIRE RIDER LIMITED

Above : Heavily cannibalised after being used for spares by Bradford depot, Bristol VRT 1730 stands in the gloom of the company's Hammerton Street premises on 12 August 1989 between a pair of Shipley Hoppa Iveco minibuses.

Left : The only Yorkshire Rider minibus transferred to West Yorkshire to carry the latter's fleet names was Freight Rover Sherpa 1765 which is seen here on 2 October 1989 passing through Bolton Woods on the 677 service to Shipley Glen.

Freight Rover Sherpa 1773, transferred from Yorkshire Rider to West Yorkshire and operated from Otley depot stands at the Guiseley terminus of Aireborough's local A1 service on 8 January 1990.

depot on 1 September, but after only a brief stay it was transferred to Hammerton Street depot, Bradford eight days later for use by West Yorkshire on Shipley Hoppa duties. Meanwhile, a further two Yorkshire Rider Sherpas had been despatched to Otley on 5 September for use on local services in that town and at Ilkley and, like 1765, these retained Yorkshire Rider livery and fleet names although all three gained West Yorkshire legal lettering vinyls. A further Freight Rover Sherpa to be transferred to the newly-acquired subsidiary was 1775 which took up its duties at Hammerton Street depot, Bradford on 12 September. On this occasion,

Yorkshire Rider Bradford's Roe-bodied Leyland Atlantean 6031 leaves Vicar Lane bus station, Leeds on a West Yorkshire Leeds depot duty on the 735 service to Otley.

although it retained its Yorkshire Rider cream & green livery, its MicroRider fleet names were replaced by traditional underlined gold West Yorkshire transfers.

By now the short term borrowing of vehicles from the parent company was becoming common place and by mid-September it was not unusual to find Roe-bodied Atlanteans of Yorkshire Rider undertaking occasional journeys on West Yorkshire services. Towards the end of that month however, a pair of Huddersfield district Roe Atlanteans appeared on schools duties from Roseville Road depot, Leeds and on 1 October, both were officially transferred to West Yorkshire and, although retaining Yorkshire Rider Huddersfield fleet names and cream & green livery, each had their legal lettering changed to reflect this move. Yet another Sherpa minibus was 'acquired' from Yorkshire Rider at this same time, this being allocated to Leeds depot by whom it was used as a staff shuttle bus between Vicar Lane bus station and Roseville Road depot. In order to eliminate the duplication of fleet numbers and place vehicles in their correct series for each type, Yorkshire Rider renumbered the whole of its newly--acquired fleet on 10 September, although in the case of the Bristol VRTs this only involved the removal of the '1' prefix from their West Yorkshire numbers.

Elsewhere in the AJS Group, Keighley & District received a Leyland Lynx demonstrator for evaluation on 4 September, but as it was not fitted with the company's standard ticketing equipment it was confined to schools and contract duties throughout the duration of its week's stay. On this same date, an NCME-bodied Leyland Leopard was hired from Hyndburn Transport, remaining with the company for four days, and this too was for the same reason restricted to schools journeys. On the penultimate day of this month, yet another stranger appeared in Keighley in the form of a Reeve Burgess-bodied Leyland Swift demonstrator, and this spent a week operating various town services before returning to its owner on 6 October. As a result of taking over the whole of

Transferred from Yorkshire Rider to West Yorkshire but still sporting MicroRider fleet names, Freight Rover Sherpa minibus 1880 stands in Templar Street, Leeds on the perimeter of Vicar Lane bus station on 12 January 1990 after having surprisingly worked a journey on the X84 service from Otley.

Sporting a West Yorkshire fleet name but with a Yorkshire Rider fleet number, Tilling red & cream-liveried Leyland National 1335 makes its way from Roseville Road, Leeds depot to Vicar Lane bus station on 30 March 1990.

Glenn Coaches ex.City of Oxford Leyland Leopard PJO8T leaves York railway station on the service to Wiggington and Haxby which operates in competition to York City & District.

the operation of the Bradford services from 13 August, Keighley vehicles were now involved in high 'dead' mileages with several having to travel 'not on service' to and from Bradford each day at the start and finish of their duties. It was not long however before slight revisions were made to the routes concerned to eliminate these wasteful journeys and make them revenue-earning. Meanwhile, York City & District cancelled the registration of their service 87 from York District Hospital to Tadcaster on 3 September, this being replaced on the following day by a new service bearing

Although seen here after being renumbered 361, this Olympian originally 1815 was Keighley & District's first dual purpose-seated vehicle to receive that company's new chinchilla & red livery. It is seen here approaching Bradford Interchange on 9 April 1990.

this same number operated by Glenn Coaches of Wiggington from the latter suburb of York to Tadcaster.

Following rumours which had been circulating for several weeks, Keighley & District finally unveiled its new livery and logo on 18 September when Leyland National 1016 and Olympian 1815 made their debut painted in chinchilla (grey) with red relief and narrow blue bands. Although it cannot be said that this was unattractive, it did however resemble undercoat or primer to a certain extent and was not what many had expected. Also undergoing repaint into these same colours at this time was 1844, one of the coach-seated Olympians, indicating that there was to be no livery differential between stage carriage and dual purpose vehicles in the future. On the same day that this new livery was launched, a 16-seat Carlyle-bodied Ford Transit arrived on loan from East Yorkshire Motor Services and although this was intended basically for use for driver training purposes, it did however occasionally stray onto Keighley's Hoppa services. Prior to this, another temporary visitor to the town arrived on 4 September when an NCME-bodied Leyland Leopard was hired from Hyndburn Transport. Painted in a white livery with red band, this was only used on that day on schools services, although it remained with the company until the 8th when it returned to Accrington.

All-white liveried Iveco minibus G150MMA spent a considerable time on loan from its manufacturer to Yorks City & District with whom it is seen here at Bishopthorpe in the twilight of a December day in 1989.

East Yorkshire Carlyle-bodied Ford Transit 307 was loaned to Keighley & District for a brief period in the autumn of 1989 and is pictured here on one of its rare appearances in revenue-earning service.

Following the departure of a large number of their coaches to the new Yorkshire Voyager concern, Northern Rose found themselves on occasions in the difficult position of not having sufficient coaches with which to operate their excursions and minibreaks. In order to maintain their programme, coaches and drivers were hired from Hutchinsons of Husthwaite for these duties as demand dictated and this caused much unrest amongst Keighley & District drivers who felt that they were being denied this type of work due to the company's lack of foresight.

York City & District unusually enjoyed a month of few changes, although this situation was to be but a brief respite. During the final days of September, a Carlyle-bodied Ford Transit was received on loan from East Yorkshire Motor Services and also joining the fleet, albeit on a temporary basis, was an all-white liveried Pheonix-bodied Iveco 19-seat demonstrator. Seven new Pheonix-bodied Ivecos made their debut on 1 October, all wearing the attractive cream & blue colors of the York undertaking and coinciding with their arrival, a large number of the city's services underwent revision. Another temporary stranger to the York City fleet made a brief appearance for a couple of days on 19 October when an open-top ex.Thames Valley Bristol FLF6G Lodekka was hired from competitors Jorvic Tours for driver training duties. More surprisingly however was the sale by York City & District of their City Tour operation to Stratford upon Avon-based Guide Friday who were already well established in this type of work in several other tourist areas around Britain. Under this deal, Guide Friday agreed to use York City's Barbican Road depot as their operating base and for maintenance purposes and were to purchase vehicles from the company for operation on the City Tour. Although one of York City's closed-top Bristol VRTs was immediately repainted into Guide Friday's green & cream livery and lettered appropriately, it continued to operate on a York City & District disc pending the granting of a new licence to Guide Friday.

Back at Keighley a shortage of conventional single deckers towards the end of October led to the company hiring two

Above : Competing with Guide Friday on York's city tours is Yorvik who since the mid 'eighties have operated open top double deckers in the city. Former Strathclyde Buses Alexander-bodied Atlantean MDS687P passes York's railway station on a wet day in June 1990.

Right : One of two Duple 320-bodied Leyland Tigers bought new by West Yorkshire, C64CYG (formerly 2415 in the West Yorkshire fleet) like its sister was sold to Yorkshire Voyager upon its formation in 1989. Freshly repainted in National Express Rapide livery, it approaches Bradford Interchange on 26 April 1990 to take up its duty on the 561 service to London.

South Wales Transport Leyland Nationals which arrived on the final day of the month. Not being equipped with Keighley & District's ticketing system, they were to be confined to schools duties for the duration of their brief stay which ended in mid-November. Another stranger to the town was a Robin Hood-bodied Iveco minibus which sported Ulsterbus fleet names, a remnant of its earlier evaluation with that operator. Arriving during the middle of October, the purpose of its loan was to allow Keighley's own Ivecos to be returned one at at time to their manufacturer for engine modifications to their pistons and liners and it quickly became a familiar sight on various of the town's Hoppa services. Meanwhile, the East Yorkshire Ford Transit, its duties completed, was returned to its owners on the last day of October.

By now, Yorkshire Rider's West Yorkshire operations appeared to have settled down and although inter-company short term loans were still occurring, fewer were witnessed in October than had taken place during the previous month. On 2 October however, a Plaxton-bodied dual-purpose Leyland Leopard was transferred from Yorkshire Rider's Gold Rider fleet at Halifax to Hammerton Street depot, Bradford and in the process was repainted into an all-over deep cream livery to which red West Yorkshire fleet names were added. The first new service to be added to the West Yorkshire operations since its passage to Yorkshire Rider was inaugurated on 29 October, numbered 627 and running from Thornton to Shipley.

Harrogate & District which had been comparatively quiet for some months received a green & white-liveried Robin Hood-bodied Iveco demonstrator on 12 October, placing this in service at Wetherby depot from where it was used on several routes until its return to its owners towards the end of that month.

The disposal of the company's former properties continued to feature in the news throughout October and despite ongoing rumours of the pending closure of Harrogate bus station, a further six months extension of its lease was gained from its new owners, Ladbrokes, thus ensuring its continued use until March 1990. Less pleasing to its owners was the rejection by Harrogate District Council of an application to build 90 starter homes on the site of Grove Park depot, Harrogate which at that time was still being used to accommodate the Harrogate & District fleet. An application made by Parkdale to demolish the bus station at Knaresborough for redevelopment also met with a cool reception from Harrogate Council, but more surprisingly was the appearance early in November of a sign at Wetherby bus station/depot stating 'Acquired by the Techno Group' which led one to believe that Parkdale had sold this without having gained planning permission. West Yorkshire Road Car Co's former head office at Sheepscar Court, Leeds, which had not been included in the sale to Rider Holdings was now regarded as a Keighley & District property and temporarily became their head office, whilst at York the York City & District travel office in Rougier Street was vacated on 30 October since when it was staffed entirely by Tourist Office personnel, its replacement being a tiny room in an adjoining alley.

Within the first few days of November, all three operating companies had placed new vehicles in service with a further Pheonix-bodied Iveco minibus joining York City & District; a Reeve Burgess dual purpose 31-seat Renault S75 making its debut with Harrogate & District and four Leyland Lynx buses taking up their duties at Keighley. The Harrogate Renault was one of a pair ordered by that company and had been exhibited at the Coach & Bus Exhibition at the NEC, Birmingham during October. The Keighley Lynxes were the first new buses to be purchased by that company since its formation and were part of an order for eight, the remainder of which entered service towards the end of the month. Wearing Keighley & District's new chinchilla & red livery, the shade of grey differing slightly from that already applied to other vehicles in the fleet as a result of being spray painted

210, one of York City & District's Pheonix-bodied Iveco minibuses in its operator's attractive cream & blue livery stands at Station Rise, York while operating a local service.

rather than brushed and the first two to enter service were fitted with electronic dot matrix destination equipment whilst the remaining six had conventional destination blinds. Surprisingly these new buses were given fleet numbers 201-8 which did not at that time fit into the company's existing numbering scheme inherited from West Yorkshire.

Following the vacation of part of their central repair works and offices in Harrogate during the previous months, an auction was arranged by ABC Parts Ltd. for the disposal of a wide range of items including workshop equipment, office furniture, mechanical and body parts and obsolete ticket machines etc. Held on 23 November in Grove Park depot, Harrogate, a number of vehicles were also included in the sale comprising 8 Keighley & District Bristol VRTs; 10 South Wales Transport Bristol VRTs; the 2 South Wales Leyland Nationals which had been on loan to Keighley & District, a Barford Atom snow plough and a former West Yorkshire Leyland National owned by Bradford Metropolitan District Council who had converted it into a mobile recruitment

office. Although bidding was brisk and almost all the sundry equipment was sold, several of the buses offered for sale - including two of the Keighley & District VRTs - failed to reach their reserve and were consequently retained by their owners. Immediately prior to this event, the EYMS Group had sold their share in ABC Parts Ltd. to the WY Group and following the auction, ABC ceased to function - although it continued to exist on paper and was not finally wound up until the summer of 1990.

Pictured on its bodybuilders stand at the Coach & Bus Exhibition at the NEC, Birmingham on 21 October 1989 is Harrogate & District Reeve Burgess Beaver-bodied Renault S75 midibus 291.

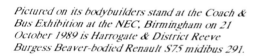

Keighley & District Leyland Lynx 202 stands in Keighley bus station in January 1990, its electronic dot matrix destination screen being set to Keighley Haworth in preparation for its next journey on route 720.

Still evaluating various types of buses, Harrogate & District received an Optare Delta-bodied DAF on loan on 21 November and put it to work on the prestigious Leeds - Harrogate - Ripon service before tranferring it to York City & District four days later. Despite finding this vehicle satisfactory, no orders have been placed for this model to date and as far as new full-sized stage carriage vehicles are concerned, the Leyland Lynx has continued to reign supreme within the North of England Travel Group.

Early November saw the emergence of a new competitor in York when Premier of Dunnington launched a fleet of ten new Reeve Burgess-bodied Renault S56 minibuses on a new service (numbered 50) between Foxwood Lane, Acomb and Osbaldwick in competition with York City & District. Finished in a dark green & cream livery and using the fleet name Target Travel, these 23-seaters operated on a high frequency basis and immediately posed a threat to the established undertaking.

The era of the Bristol Lodekka with West Yorkshire Road Car Co. Ltd. which had begun in June 1950 with the receipt of one of the prototypes had finally come to a close on 12 August when the last two remaining examples used in the driver training fleet were sold to Yorkshire Rider. Although these continued to reside on West Yorkshire property at Roseville Road depot, Leeds, neither were used by their new owner and both were eventually sold on 24 November to Mayday Contract Services of Leeds for whom it was believed that they would continue in use as driver tuition vehicles. Joining these at Roseville Road depot towards the end of October was yet another Lodekka, this being the previously preserved ex.York West Yorkshire YDX221 which had most surprisingly also been sold to Mayday. This has however happily been resold for preservation to a Bradford-based group who intend to maintain it as a West Yorkshire vehicle rather than one from erstwhile joint York undertaking.

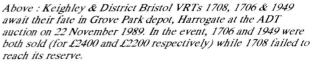

Above : Keighley & District Bristol VRTs 1708, 1706 & 1949 await their fate in Grove Park depot, Harrogate at the ADT auction on 22 November 1989. In the event, 1706 and 1949 were both sold (for £2400 and £2200 respectively) while 1708 failed to reach its reserve.

December 1989 saw the arrival of the second of the two new Reeve Burgess-bodied Renault S75 midibuses for Harrogate & District and like its sister, it was fitted with dual purpose-type seats. Allocated to Pateley Bridge outstation, it became a regular performer on the services connecting that Dales township with Harrogate previously maintained by conventional single deckers. Harrogate Independent Travel

Above : A reminder of the past is preserved former York West Yorkshire Bristol FS6B Lodekka 3821 of 1966 vintage.. Having recently changed ownership, it is now intended to retain this vehicle as a pseudo-West Yorkshire bus and to number it 1821.

Left : Target Travel began operations in York in competition to York City & District in November 1989 using a fleet of ten new NCME-bodied Renault minibuses. One of these, G255LWF heads along Station Road on its way to Foxwood Lane on 23 November 1989.

Harrogate & District Reeve Burgess Beaver-bodied Renault S75 291 leaves Harrogate bus station on 22 May 1990 on the 24 service to Pateley Bridge.

Withdrawn behind Harrogate & District's Grove Park depot on 22 May 1990 are Harrogate Independent Travel Caetano-bodied Bedford UTG313S and ex.London Transport Daimler Fleetline KWU410N which, when in service had been registered GHV1N.

also gained an additional pair of vehicles, both of which were transferred from the Keighley & District fleet. One of these was a Bristol VRT, this doubling the company's double deck total, the other being a dual purpose Plaxton-bodied Leyland Leopard. As a result of not yet having had their application for an increased number of licences granted, both these new additions were officially owned by York City & District whose legal lettering they carried and on whose discs they were operated during their first few weeks in service from Starbeck. The Bristol VRT carried Tilling red & cream livery complete with York City & District fleet names whilst the Leopard sported Northern Rose colours from which the lettering had been removed.

The temporary arrangement with Guide Friday continued at York pending the granting to the latter of their new licence and as a short-term measure, a former City of Nottingham Willowbrook-bodied open-top Daimler Fleetline of Guide Friday was acquired by York City & District for use on the York City Tour alongside closed-top Bristol VRT 1984 which still remained in the ownership of the York undertaking despite it wearing Friday's green & cream livery etc. Both these buses were 'officially' acquired by Guide Friday in January upon the receipt of their new operator's licence. Adding to the variety in this historic city was a new double deck livery introduced by York City & District on one of their Yorkshire Coastliner dual-purpose seated Leyland

Guide Friday temporarily transferred one of their open top ex.Nottingham Daimler Fleetlines to York during the latter part of 1989, operating this on a York City & District disc pending the granting of their own licence. The bus concerned, ETO161L is seen here in August 1989 at Waverley Bridge, Edinburgh whilst working on Guide Friday's tours of that city.

Painted in Yorkshire Rider livery but wearing West Yorkshire fleet names, ex.Sovereign Bus & Coach Roe-bodied Atlantean 6430 leaves Vicar Lane bus station, Leeds at the start of its journey to Bradford on route 670 on 30 March 1990. As can be seen, it still lacked a destination blind at this time.

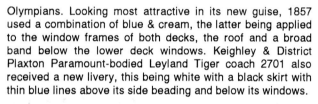

Arriving in Knaresborough from Leeds on the 796 service on 21 June 1989 is York City & District's all-over advertising liveried Bristol VRT 1740 which on that occasion was operating from Wetherby depot.

Olympians. Looking most attractive in its new guise, 1857 used a combination of blue & cream, the latter being applied to the window frames of both decks, the roof and a broad band below the lower deck windows. Keighley & District Plaxton Paramount-bodied Leyland Tiger coach 2701 also received a new livery, this being white with a black skirt with thin blue lines above its side beading and below its windows.

Having already acquired a large quantity of secondhand double deckers from Greater Manchester Buses in 1987/8, Yorkshire Rider ventured into the used vehicle market again in November 1989 with the purchase of twelve Roe-bodied Leyland Atlanteans from Sovereign Bus & Coach Co. of Hatfield, Herts, (formerly London Country North East), another member of the AJS Group. Although not known at that time, all twelve of these buses were to be allocated to Rider's West Yorkshire subsidiary and despite being painted in Yorkshire Rider's standard cream & green livery, the first to enter service - 6433 on 6 December - was given large red West Yorkshire fleet names. Allocated to Roseville Road depot, Leeds it was joined mid-month by 6430 which similarly sported West Yorkshire fleet names etc. During their first weeks in service these new acquisitions wandered onto most of Leeds depot's routes and reached Bradford, Ilkley and Otley on several occasions.

Meanwhile, the disposal or attempted disposal of former West Yorkshire properties continued, almost with indecent haste, and during December a sign was erected outside Hammerton Street depot, Bradford offering its 52,000 sq.ft. of buildings and adjacent parking yard for sale at an asking price of around £750,000. At Leeds, planning permission had been applied for by Barr and Wallace Arnold Trust to convert Roseville Road depot into a car showroom and garage/workshop whilst at York it was leaked that Barbican Road depot was to be closed and its inhabitants dispersed to four locations on the fringe of the city. Press reports also suggested that Wetherby depot was to close early in 1990 and in preparation for this and the pending closure of Grove Park depot at Harrogate, Harrogate & District had purchased the former Reynard Pullman premises at Manse Lane, Knaresborough. Due to its size however, this would be inadequate to accommodate the whole of the Harrogate & District fleet and it was therefore planned to use it only for the company's conventional buses and those displaced at Wetherby, the minibuses being housed at the Harrogate Independent Travel base at Starbeck. Despite rumours suggesting that Grove Park was to close on 31 December, due to the alterations being carried out at Manse Lane taking longer than had been originally anticipated, the depot still remained in use until the early summer of 1990. Following an application made by AJS Holdings for flats and bungalows to be built on the site of Grassington depot/bus station - which was still being used for its intended purpose - Keighley &

Leaving Vicar Lane bus station, Leeds on a 796 journey on the Leeds - Wetherby corridor on 30 March 1990 is Plaxton-bodied Leyland Leopard 1546 which was to lose its West Yorkshire fleet names two days later upon its transfer to Yorkshire Rider's Halifax division.

District began a search for an alternative site in that area from which to operate their vehicles, but as will be seen later, this did not materialise. Finally, at Knaresborough where the bus station had already been vacated and buses now picked up and set down in the already heavily-congested streets, Harrogate Council confirmed a new traffic control order which prohibited buses from collecting or depositing their passengers in High Street and Fisher Street. This immediately upset Harrogate & District who took legal advice and considered applying for a judicial review.

Despite a number of minor modifications being made to the services of Harrogate & District and Yorkshire Rider (West Yorkshire) operating on the Leeds - Wetherby - Knaresborough corridor, there still remained a vast amount of wasteful duplication which, at its most ridiculous, saw a Harrogate & District 797 Wetherby - Kirk Deighton and 796 Wetherby - Kirk Deighton - Knaresborough journey together with a West Yorkshire 796 Leeds - Wetherby - Kirk Deighton vehicle all leave Wetherby within the space of four minutes. It was highly unlikely that there would ever be sufficient passengers between Wetherby and Kirk Deighton to fill one bus, let alone three. This incidentally was the only instance where competition existed between West Yorkshire (Yorkshire Rider) and any of its former associated companies and through further timetable changes, this ludicrous situation was finally eliminated in the spring of 1990. Following the departure of West Yorkshire from the AJS stable, Explorer Tickets issued by Harrogate & District, Keighley & District and York City & District were no longer valid on West Yorkshire (Yorkshire Rider) services.

The never well used Keighley & District 759 service (Keighley to Guiseley) was withdrawn after operation on 23 December whilst on Christmas Day Keighley & District operated two buses on a restricted service on the 663 route

from Oxenhope to Bradford and one on the 700 service from Silsden to Haworth. In complete contrast, York City & District did not operate any vehicles on 24, 25, 26 and 31 December or on New Year's Day 1990. To compensate for this, competitor Target Travel took over service 9 from Osbaldwick to Clifton on 24 and 31 December at short notice with the support of York City Council. Also, in addition to maintaining their local services in York during the Christmas period, Reynard Pullman also temporarily stepped in (at the request of York City Council) to run three return journeys from York to Leeds on the 843 service on Christmas Eve and New Year's Eve.

The anticipated expansion of Harrogate Independent Travel came to fruition in the days around the turn of the year when on 28 December they began operation of service 14 from Wetherby to Pannal and on 3 January 1990 took over the Reynard Pullman services in and around Harrogate following the decision by the latter to withdraw from the area. Three former Pullman Leyland Leopards and an NCME-bodied dual purpose-seated Renault S56 minibus were acquired by Challenger who further expanded their fleet by the addition of a Plaxton-bodied dual purpose Leyland Leopard from York City & District and another Bristol VRT from Keighley & District. A new Reeve Burgess-bodied Renault S56 was also purchased and added to their growing fleet during January. The three ex. Pullman Leopards and the Bristol VRT were all given an all-over white livery whilst the York City Leopard retained its Tilling red & cream colours which were adorned with both its previous and new owners fleet names. Due to Harrogate Independent Travel's increased licence application still not having been received, it was necessary to licence the new acquisitions to York City & District whose legal lettering they carried until 26 January when Challenger's additional authorisation was gained. Their

Awaiting its Knaresborough-bound passengers in Station Parade, Harrogate outside the town's bus station on 22 May 1990 is Harrogate Independent Travel UWA91S, a Duple-bodied Leopard acquired from Reynard Pullman at the start of the year.

Below : Acquired by Harrogate Independent Travel from Reynard Pullman of York, NCME-bodied Dodge S56 E194HFV is seen here in its new owner's white & blue livery traversing Station Parade, Harrogate on its way to Bilton.

Below. Reynard Pullman's NPA226W, a Plaxton-bodied Leyland Leopard started life as a Green Line coach in the fleet of London Country Bus Services Ltd.

Freshly repainted in Yorkshire Rider's colours and standing in West Yorkshire's Roseville Road, Leeds depot on 30 March 1990 is Bristol VRT 988 which already carried Yorkshire Rider Wakefield fleet names in preparation for its transfer to its new owner's Kinsley depot.

Hurrying towards Otley on a 654 journey from Bradford on 7 March 1990, Leyland National 1343 although already having received Yorkshire Rider livery and side fleet names carried a West Yorkshire title below its windscreens.

Bradford depot's first Bristol VRT to receive Yorkshire Rider's cream & green livery was 744 which remained unique in being the only VRT in its new master's colours to carry West Yorkshire fleet names. It is seen here on 9 April 1990 leaving Bradford Interchange on a 670 journey to Leeds.

Opposite page :

Left column, top to bottom :

Still wearing its West Yorkshire blue Hoppa livery, albeit with Yorkshire Rider fleet names, Robin Hood-bodied Iveco 2064 arrives at the Horton Bank Top terminus of Bradford cross-city service 847 on 6 June 1990.

One of Keighley & District's Leyland Lynx single deckers, 205 climbs Bridge Street, Bradford enroute to the Interchange in February 1990 whilst operating on the Bradford - Keighley - Skipton corridor.

Keighley & District's former County Bus & Coach Co. Olympian 379 (B268LPH) rather than being repainted into its new owner's chinchilla & red colours had the green areas of its former operator's livery repainted red to resemble Keighley's own dual purpose-seated Olympians. It is seen here in Bradford.

This 1987 view of West Yorkshire Bristol VRT 1741 climbing Hollins Hill twoards Guiseley on route 755 shows it still wearing NBC poppy red livery and NBC-style fleet name.

Right column, top to bottom :

Harrogate & District Leyland National 363 rests on the forecourt of Grove Park depot, Harrogate on 22 May 1990, eight days before the closure of these premises.

York City & District Robin Hood-bodied Iveco 209 looks immaculate in its attractive cream & blue livery as it stops opposite York railway station in the spring of 1989.

One of the Roe-bodied Leyland Atlanteans purchased by Yorkshire Rider from AJS Group subsidiary Sovereign Bus & Coach Co., 6433 (KPJ291W) although painted in Yorkshire Rider colours was given West Yorkshire fleet names. It is seen here in Vicar Lane, Leeds on 12 January 1990 soon after its entry into service.

Fitted with a new Plaxton front and re-registered AEG984A, Leyland Leopard 2588 seen here in Keighley bus station on 20 April 1989 was finished in the attractive blue Northern Rose coaching livery.

new services took the company into several areas new to them including Wetherby and Otley and in addition to the services taken over from Reynard Pullman they also gained several contracts from that operator in addition to winning a number by their own efforts. Harrogate & District withdrew completely from service 56 Harrogate - Ripon (schools) and 57 Harrogate - Roecliffe, passing these to United for rationalisation purposes.

Above left : Cream & green liveried former West Yorkshire Bristol VRT 741 pictured at Shipley on 3 March 1990 had its Yorkshire Rider fleet name incorrectly applied with the YR logo to the rear of the offside instead of at the front. Additionally, no district name was carried. (J.Cass)

Above : Still wearing Tilling red & cream livery and featuring the original-style Keighley & District fleet name, Olympian 352 climbs Bridge Street, Bradford enroute to the Interchange on 9 April 1990, its destination blind having already been re-set in preparation for its return to Skipton.

Left : Although still retaining its Tilling red livery, Keighley & District Bristol VRT 313 had received a chinchilla band and grey fleet name panel when caught by the camera outside Keighley bus station on 10 May 1990.

After pulling out of services in the Harrogate area, Reynard Pullman began three new commercially registered routes in York on 2 January from South Bank to Bishopthorpe Road, to Heworth and to Ashley Park. Numbered 14, 11 and 12 respectively, these used conventional sized buses and offered York City & District even more competition in their established surrounds. The growing threat from predators in York was however quickly reduced when the AJS Group acquired a controlling interest in Target Travel during January. This company, like Harrogate Independent Travel, was however to retain its autonomy and although all Target's stage carriage operations and minibus fleet were included in the deal, the company's former owner, Brian Gallier who remained as manager following the passage of control to AJS, retained his Premier coaching interests which he hoped to expand in the future. In addition to their nine Reeve Burgess-Renault minibuses (the tenth had already been withdrawn in December after being burnt out), Target were also operating a Reeve Burgess-bodied Mercedes demonstrator which had been on loan since late December. The Target fleet was still operated from its original premises at Pearsons Garage, Gate Helmsley on the fringe of the city and retained its dark green & cream livery.

Harrogate & District 275, a Reeve Burgess-bodied Iveco 25-seat minibus stands in Harrogate bus station on 14 April 1990. The sticker in the lower corner of its windscreen proclaims that new fares are in operation. (J.Whitmore)

COASTLINER GAINS AUTONOMY

Further changes within the North of England Travel Group saw the divorce of Malton depot's activities from York City & District on 2 January when a new company under the title of Yorkshire Coastliner Ltd. was set up to take over all Malton's operations. Five dual purpose Leyland Leopards and four dual purpose Olympians were transferred from York City & District to the new company who took over the operation of services 92, 824, 843, 844, 879 and X43. Five new Plaxton Paramount-bodied Leyland Tiger coaches were immediately ordered by Coastliner and it was intended that upon their arrival in the late spring, they would replace the Olympians which would then be cascaded back to York. Finally, the Ford Transit minibus which had been on loan from East Yorkshire since September 1989 was purchased by York City in January 1990, still wearing its previous owner's livery and carrying their Skipper fleet names.

The West Yorkshire fleet continued to receive ex.Sovereign Bus & Coach Roe-bodied Atlanteans as these made their debut during January and although two of these appeared with West Yorkshire fleet names added to their cream & green livery, two others had Yorkshire Rider Leeds names but carried West Yorkshire legal lettering. Their entry into service at Roseville Road, Leeds allowed the withdrawal of a couple of West Yorkshire's Bristol VRTs, one of which on 3 January was transferred to Yorkshire Rider's Wakefield

Looking immaculate in its attractive Yorkshire Coastliner livery, dual purpose Leyland Olympian 1855 passes York railway station enroute from Scarborough to Leeds.

Helping out on West Yorkshire's Otley town service 778 is Yorkshire Rider Freight Rover Sherpa 1755 in its owner's Micro Rider livery.

area depot at Kinsley still in Tilling red & cream livery. Another bus of this type (994) was first repainted into standard Yorkshire Rider colours and given YR Wakefield names before joining 752 at Kinsley early in February for use mainly on schools contract duties. At around this same time, a surprise instruction issued by Yorkshire Rider to Hammerton Street depot, Bradford stated that of the two Bristol VRTs scheduled for imminent repainting, one had to be finished in Tilling red & cream, the other in Yorkshire Rider cream & green and that all subsequent repaints were to be in standard Rider colours. Following discussion between a number of staff at that depot, it was decided that 765, which had worked West Yorkshire's final journey on 12 August, should be outshopped in Tilling red and that 744 was therefore to receive the new cream & green colour scheme. Both vehicles surprisingly received West Yorkshire fleet names whereas Leeds depot's first repaint into cream & green - Bristol VRT 973 - was given Yorkshire Rider Leeds fleet names. Adding to the identity saga, the first Leyland National to be transformed into the colours of its new master was Bradford depot's 1343 which emerged on 12 January with Yorkshire Rider fleet names on each side which omitted an area identification and a red West Yorkshire name at the front below its windscreens. Confused. . . then read on.

During the days leading up to the final absorption of West Yorkshire, Yorkshire Rider vehicles were as common on West Yorkshire routes as were red buses. This scene in Vicar Lane bus station, Leeds on 30 March 1990 shows West Yorkshire red Bristol VRT 987 resting alongside Yorkshire Rider Roe-bodied Atlantean 6309 and one of the ex.Sovereign Bus & Coach Co. examples, 6428.

Temporary loans of Yorkshire Rider buses to West Yorkshire depots became familiar during the autumn of 1989 and spring of 1990. On this occasion, Roe-bodied Atlantean 6230 is seen leaving Vicar Lane bus station, Leeds on a journey to Ilkley on West Yorkshire route 733.

The first West Yorkshire Leyland Olympian to receive Yorkshire Rider livery was 5189 illustrated at Vicar Lane bus station, Leeds whilst working route 767 to Shadwell.

Opposite page.

Left column, top to bottom :

Seen leaving Bradford Interchange on 5 April 1990 on Yorkshire Rider service 637 to Bradford Moor is former West Yorkshire Leyland Olympian 5199, still in its original owner's Tilling red & cream livery but sporting Yorkshire Rider fleet name vinyls.

Ex.County Bus & Coach Co. ECW-bodied Leyland Olympian LR69 was hired by Keighley & District for evaluation in May 1990. Still wearing its County livery, but having had Keighley & District fleet names and logos applied, it is seen here enroute to Bradford on route 664 on 23 May 1990, a few days before it was purchased and repainted into its new owner's standard chinchilla & red colours.

Keighley & District Duple-bodied Leyland Leopard 231 is seen here on 23 May 1990 wearing its modified Northern Rose livery after the replacement of its red areas with white. It is interesting to compare this picture with that of this same vehicle on page 17.

Yorkshire Rider Huddersfield Roe-bodied Leyland Atlantean 6350 still painted in the old West Yorkshire PTE livery of Verona green & buttermilk is seen in Templar Street, Leeds on 22 September 1989 whilst on hire to West Yorkshire for use on school contract duties.

Right column, top to bottom :

Following its transfer from Harrogate & District to York City & District, Leyland Lynx 7 at first retained its former owner's cream & red livery and merely gained York fleet names and numbers. It is seen in this form in Station Road, York whilst working city service 7 on 2 June 1990.

Two days before the official complete absorption of West Yorkshire by Yorkshire Rider, Plaxton Paramount bodied dual purpose Leyland Tiger 1624 had already gained its new owner's fleet name vinyls as can be seen as it leaves Vicar Lane bus station, Leeds enroute to Otley on route 736 on 30 March 1990.

Re-numbered 1549 by Yorkshire Rider, this Duple-bodied Leyland Leopard pictured in Vicar Lane bus station, Leeds on 22 September 1989 sported new-style West Yorkshire fleet names incorporating a large W and similar-sized Y.

Despite wearing National Express corporate livery and displaying Northern Rose fleet names, Plaxton Paramount-bodied Leyland Tiger 2703 was operating a stage carriage duty on the 760 service to Keighley when caught by the camera at Vicar Lane bus station, Leeds on 25 May 1989. This coach later passed to the newly-formed Yorkshire Voyager company along with West Yorkshire's National Express operations.

Despite having introduced their own new livery of chinchilla with red relief during the autumn of 1989, Keighley & District decided to repaint their Bristol VRTs into Tilling red with a chinchilla centre band, perhaps due to this type of vehicle having but a short life expectancy with the company. Following this, rather than completely repaint the VRTs, a programme was set up to repaint only the cream band into the new chinchilla shade and this was completed by mid-April. In the interim period, most of the Keighley fleet received new destnation blinds which were printed black on yellow and although some vehicles also received matching route number blinds, others retained their old white on black numerals. Before this transformation had been completed, the whole of the Keighley & District fleet with the exception of the Iveco minibuses was renumbered during the night of 27/28 January. The system adopted was irrational to say the least, and no attempt was made to segregate coach-seated vehicles from the standard stage carriage types. Even more inexplicable was the renumbering of the open-top Bristol VRT (658) into the ancillary vehicle series (40), thus continuing to keep it apart from all its sisters.

During the gales which swept the country in January 1990, the main doors at Grove Park depot, Harrogate were damaged by the high winds and until such times as repairs could be undertaken, withdrawn Bristol VRT 1716 was used as a temporary door to keep out the worst of the elements. Its use in this unusual manner continued for several days until the weather eased and the original doors were able to be made sound and brought back into use.

By now, Yorkshire Voyager had finally moved out of Hammerton Street depot, Bradford to their new premises off Kirkstall Road, Leeds but had left behind an immobile MCW Metroliner. This had been heavily cannibalised and needed a considerable amount of work to enable it to leave Bradford depot and it was several more weeks before it eventually departed. By this time an 'Under Offer' sign had appeared outside Bradford depot whilst rumours abounded that these premises along with the depots at Roseville Road, Leeds and Bondgate, Otley had to be vacated by the end of February. This, like many other rumours circulating at that time proved to be incorrect, as will be seen later. Meanwhile, despite the depot at Pateley Bridge having vanished, the adjacent bus station continued in use surrounded by new building work whilst at Ilkley the former depot had finally been demolished only to reveal the remains of what was believed to be an old

Roman road. As a result of this discovery, archaeologists asked Bradford Council's planning department to have work on the construction of an arcade of Victorian-style shops on the site delayed to allow them more time to investigate.

February witnessed both arrivals and departures within the associated fleets and amongst these was the termination of the loan of Iveco minibus D274SMA to Keighley & District and the withdrawal of three of that company's Bristol VRTs. Harrogate & District received the first two of a batch of six new 25-seat Reeve Burgess-bodied Iveco minibuses (275/6) whilst Harrogate Independent Travel repainted their two Tilling red & cream-liveried vehicles - a Bristol VRT and a dual purpose Leyland Leopard - into the all-over white which appeared to have become that company's standard colour scheme. Still on the subject of liveries, despite having already painted one of their dual-purpose Olympians into their new blue & cream colours, York City & District transformed another of their vehicles of this type into cream & red. Applied in similar proportions this was apparently in preparation for this vehicle's eventual transfer to the Harrogate & District fleet. Target Travel added two new Reeve Burgess-bodied Renault S56 minibuses to their fleet and also received a Reeve Burgess-bodied Iveco demonstrator on loan whilst York City & District were still operating the all-white liveried Pheonix-bodied Iveco demonstrator which had now spent more than five months in the city. Meanwhile, Reynard Pullman, having sold the whole of their coaching operation to Kingston upon Hull City Transport were now in a position to expand their stage carriage activities and attack York City & District whenever the opportunity arose.

In preparation for the forthcoming total absorption of West Yorkshire by Yorkshire Rider, a start was made during February on the fitting of West Yorkshire vehicles with two-way radios and additionally at Bradford depot, with fare boxes. This work was undertaken at Rider's Kirkstall Road workshops, Leeds and to cover for vehicles being so equipped, several Yorkshire Rider buses were drafted into West Yorkshire depots on a temporary basis, these often changing daily. At this same time, West Yorkshire's Bradford Hoppa fleet was transferred from Hammerton Street to Yorkshire Rider's Hall Ings depot with the result that the 'Shipley Hoppa' Ivecos now began to appear on various Rider services. The repainting of West Yorkshire vehicles into cream & green continued steadily and a further two of the ex.Sovereign Atlanteans made their debut in service from Roseville Road depot, Leeds complete with Yorkshire Rider Leeds fleet names. As it was known that the West Yorkshire's Leeds-based fleet would be dispersed amongst three Yorkshire Rider depots within the city on 1 April following the closure of the Roseville Road premises, a route-learning programme was commenced for the Yorkshire Rider drivers at Bramley and Headingley depots from which the majority of the West Yorkshire services would ultimately be operated. This took vehicles such as MCW Metrobuses to the unfamiliar areas of Aireborough, Otley, Ilkley and Skipton where they provided a foretaste of what was likely to come in the not too distant future and in addition, several such sorties were also undertaken in a variety of Yorkshire Rider minibuses.

March began with the entry into service of two more of Harrogate & District's new Reeve Burgess-bodied Iveco minibuses and these were followed by the remaining pair mid-month. Target Travel placed an order for a further ten Reeve Burgess-bodied Renaults while York City & District withdrew two of its Bristol VRTs and sold them to Guide

Following its withdrawal from service by Yorkshire Rider and the removal of its fleet names and numbers in preparation for its disposal, Freight Rover Sherpa 1733 was reinstated for use by West Yorkshire as a staff shuttle bus between Vicar Lane bus station and Roseville Road depot, Leeds.

After being transferred from West Yorkshire's depot at Bradford to Yorkshire Rider's Hall Ings site, the cream & red-liveried Shipley Hoppa Iveco minibuses began to appear on Yorkshire Rider services. On this occasion, 2081 passes its old home in Hammerton Street on its way from Tyersal to Bradford city centre on route 630.

Friday. York City's two Leyland Lynx single deckers which, since their transfer from Harrogate & District had retained their former owner's cream & red livery had their red areas repainted blue and former East Yorkshire Ford Transit 305 finally gained York City & District's standard colours.

Following the inauguration by Keighley & District on 4 February of a new service from Keighley Market Street to Rainham Crescent (716), another new service was commenced on 26 March running from Market Street to Bell Square, Silsden and numbered 713. The company's name was at last shown on the bus station and depot buildings and operations in and around this town appeared to the onlooker at least, to have settled to a successful pattern. Perhaps as a result of this, approaches were made by several concerns interested in acquiring the Keighley & District company including Yorkshire Rider and Burnley & Pendle Transport, but on each occasion were given to understand that it was most definately not for sale.

Quite obviously, it was West Yorkshire Road Car Co. who stole the scene during March and as the month progressed, so the signs of the demise of this once-important company became more obvious. The final four ex.Sovereign Atlanteans drifted into service from Roseville Road, Leeds depot between 2 and 20 March with the final example being 6426. These displayed a curious mixture of identities with 6429 entering service on 2 March with Yorkshire Rider Leeds fleet names and West Yorkshire legal ownership panel followed on 12 March by 6435 which displayed West Yorkshire names and legal lettering. The remaining two, 6425 and 6426 which took up their duties on 13 and 20

March respectively both had Yorkshire Rider fleet names and legal lettering but nevertheless were wholly used on West Yorkshire services. A further addition to the West Yorkshire fleet was, surprisingly, a Freight Rover Sherpa which had been in store following its withdrawal by Yorkshire Rider several months earlier. With its fleet names and numbers already removed in preparation for its sale, 1733 was given West Yorkshire legal lettering but a Yorkshire Rider operators disc and was put to use as a staff transfer vehicle for operation between Vicar Lane bus station and Roseville Road depot, Leeds.

During its final weeks of operation, Otley depot took on a new look following the abandonment of its fixed vehicle allocation. As a result, it received a daily-changing variety of vehicles from Leeds and the most common type used were the ex. Sovereign Bus & Coach Co. Atlanteans which soon became a familiar sight on the depot forecourt and in the town's new bus station. Most of Otley's Iveco and Ford Transit minibuses also departed during the latter part of March, being replaced by Yorkshire Rider's MCW Metroriders which, fitted with new destination blinds soon settled down on their new duties on Otley and Ilkley town services. One of the pair of Plaxton Derwent-bodied Leopards transferred in August 1989 from Yorkshire Rider Halifax to West Yorkshire at Bradford was withdrawn from its duties early in the month and despatched to Kirkstall Road works for repainting into Yorkshire Rider's cream & green livery. Although not generally known at that time, this vehicle had already been sold to the Red Ladder Theatre Co. of Leeds which was apparently sponsored by Yorkshire Rider,

Towards the end of March 1990, Otley depot's Ford Transit Hoppa minibuses began to be replaced by Yorkshire Rider MCW Metroriders, one of which - 2050 - is seen leaving the bus station on the town service to Weston Estate followed by an ex.Sovereign Bus & Coach Co. Atlantean, 6429 which strangely shows 7A82 on its route number blinds.

Above : The refurbished depot at Otley during its final week of operation in March 1990 provided home for several Yorkshire Rider vehicles including a pair of MCW Metrorider minibuses and an ex.Sovereign Bus & Coach Co. Roe-bodied Leyland Atlantean seen here resting on the forecourt.

hence the reason for it being repainted into cream & green - albeit minus fleet names.

As March progressed, so the sight of Yorkshire Rider buses operating West Yorkshire services increased, particularly from Roseville Road depot, Leeds and cream & green buses became almost as familiar in places like Otley and Ilkley as were those in red livery. Over the two days 21/22 March, all West Yorkshire's vehicles and those of Yorkshire Rider in the Leeds and Bradford areas received new destination blinds in preparation for their future operation to previously unfamiliar places. Later in the month, new timetable booklets and leaflets began to appear showing the numerous service alterations which were to take place on 1 April and Metro's publicity buses visited several locations to distribute new travel guides and provide information to the travelling public in an attempt to reduce confusion when the full integration of the two companies took place. The pre-planning of these service changes had been excellent and all credit must be given to Metro and Yorkshire Rider for their efforts in this direction. Additional publicity was applied to the vehicles of both companies informing passengers that the red and green buses were now all under the same ownership.

Above : Metro's mobile information centre, converted from former West Yorkshire PTE Alexander-bodied Metrobus UWW514X, was used on the car park at Bradford Interchange at the end of March 1990 to publicise the unbelievable number of service changes taking place on 1 April following the total absorption of West Yorkshire Road Car Co. Ltd.

Tilling red & cream-liveried Bristol VRT 993, pictured here in West Yorkshire's Roseville Road depot, Leeds on 30 March 1990, has already had its fleet names covered by Yorkshire Rider Limited vinyls and has been fitted with new destination blinds for use following its transfer to Kinsley depot.

The removal of non-running vehicles from West Yorkshire's Roseville Road, Leeds depot began on 30 March 1990 in preparation for its closure the following night. Seddon Atkinson recovery vehicle 4077 is seen here towing Bristol VRT 729 out of the depot enroute to Yorkshire Rider's Kirkstall Road workshops.

Right : West Yorkshire's all-over advertising Bristol VRT 756 received Yorkshire Rider fleet name vinyls a few days before the official demise of the former. It is seen here on 30 March 1990 leaving Vicar Lane bus station, Leeds enroute to Shadwell on route 767.

Despite the date of the complete integration of West Yorkshire into the Yorkshire Rider network still being days away, several of the former's 'red' buses began to receive Yorkshire Rider Limited fleet name vinyls which obliterated their West Yorkshire identity a few days before the end of March and thus the scene was set. March 31 dawned all too soon and it was now only a matter of hours before West Yorkshire Road Car Co. Ltd. was to disappear completely and the depots at Roseville Road, Leeds; Hammerton Street, Bradford and Bondgate, Otley would close their doors for the final time. To commemorate this sad occasion, Bradford depot used Bristol VRT 733 for the final West Yorkshire journey of the day, this being on the 661 service from Baildon to Bradford Interchange and this was almost a repeat of the scene of 12 August 1989. Leeds depot selected Leyland National 1305 to perform their last rites, this arriving back at Vicar Lane bus station, Leeds from Westfield on route 738 a few minutes after midnight. The clock at Vicar Lane bus station was stopped at 11.59pm. and the end of a long era was finally reached.

Right & below : Two views of Vicar Lane bus station, Leeds on 31 March 1990, its final day of operation, showing vehicles in several different liveries.

45

THE END OF AN ERA

April 1st marked the almost total disappearance of the West Yorkshire fleet name when, during the early hours this was hidden beneath Yorkshire Rider Limited vinyls printed red on a cream background and the only survivors to carry the old company's title were the ex.Sovereign Atlanteans and Bradford's Bristol VRT 744. As these were already in Yorkshire Rider colours, it seems likely that they were overlooked when the general fleet name change took place, the staff carrying out this task obviously thinking that these already sported Yorkshire Rider identity and in the event some soldiered on for several days into April before this error was discovered.

During the week that followed, Leeds, Bradford and Otley depots were completely cleared of everything that was removable, although Hammerton Street was given a temporary reprieve with the arrival of several of Yorkshire Rider's withdrawn minibuses and a handful of West Yorkshire vehicles awaiting dispersal to other depots. Vicar Lane bus station at Leeds quickly changed its identity to become a temporary NCP car park and thus as such can loosely be said to still retain a transport connection. Leeds Central bus station now hosted many of the services previously operated from Vicar Lane and as such was used by West Yorkshire's former associates Keighley & District; Harrogate & District and Yorkshire Coastliner Ltd. Several former West Yorkshire services had now been incorporated into Yorkshire Rider routes to provide new cross-city links in Leeds, and it soon became common place to find red buses working former Rider services and conversely, cream & green buses on ex.West Yorkshire routes.

Above : An example of a red bus operating a green route, ex.West Yorkshire Leyland Olympian 5199 climbs through Clayton Heights on its way to Queensbury from Pudsey on route 610 in June 1990.

Left : An example of a green bus on a red route, Yorkshire Rider's Headingley depot MCW Metrobus 7595 approaches Yeadon on the 755 service from Leeds to Bradford in May 1990.

Below : An empty West Yorkshire Hammerton Street depot, Bradford on 2 April 1990 whilst it was being cleared of the last of its equipment and vehicles.

Although the majority of the ex.West Yorkshire vehicles remained in Yorkshire Rider's Leeds and Bradford divisions, fourteen Leyland National 2s were, early in April, transferred to Huddersfield, five dual purpose Leopards to Halifax and seven Bristol VRTs plus a pair of Leopards to Kinsley, thus taking 'red' buses to even more unfamiliar surrounds. Following the closure of the three West Yorkshire depots, the company's vehicles at Leeds were in the main transferred to Yorkshire Rider's Bramley and Headingley premises, with a tiny handful of Leyland Nationals also being reallocated to Torre Road whilst at Bradford all were moved from Hammerton Street to the large depot at Hall Ings, underneath the Interchange. At Otley, the picture was somewhat different however, for with Yorkshire Rider not having property in or near the town, a new site had to be found at which the fleet could be accommodated. This led to

The former West Yorkshire depot at Roseville Road, Leeds on 2 April following its closure two days earlier.

The last West Yorkshire vehicle to be repainted into Tilling red & cream livery was Bradford depot's Bristol VRT 765. On 1 April however, it lost its West Yorkshire fleet names in favour of Yorkshire Rider vinyls and is seen approaching Bradford Interchange nine days later on Yorkshire Rider service 616.

space being rented at the premises of demolition contractors, Ogdens of Otley in whose yard Rider's vehicles began to be stabled from 1 April. All maintenance was carried out at Headingley depot who provided an almost daily-changing allocation of conventional sized and minibuses for Otley's use, a situation which although acceptable cannot have been found to be ideal.

Some of the former West Yorkshire Leyland Leopards left their usual surrounds on 1 April for service in Yorkshire Rider's Calderdale area. One such vehicle, Tilling red & cream-liveried 1546 rests in Halifax bus station alongside one of Yorkshire Rider's ex.Greater Manchester Daimler Fleetlines on 27 April 1990.

Former Yorkshire Rider Halifax Plaxton Derwent-bodied Leyland Leopard 8515 after being transferred to West Yorkshire at Bradford depot in August 1989 and being repainted red & cream returned home to Halifax depot in April 1990. It is seen here, still in Tilling red & cream but with Yorkshire Rider fleet names resting in the town's bus station on 27 April 1990 after operating a duty on the 528 service from Rochdale.

Yorkshire Rider 5193, a former West Yorkshire Road Car Co. Ltd. Leyland Olympian was one of several to have its opening front upper deck bulkhead windows replaced by fixed glazing. Still wearing its former owner's Tilling red & cream livery, albeit with its new master's fleet name vinyls, it continued to publicise West Yorkshire's services on its side poster as it climbs Moore Avenue, Bradford on Yorkshire Rider service 634 early in June 1990.

Fitted with Yorkshire Rider Limited fleet name vinyls, blue Hoppa-liveried ex. West Yorkshire Robin Hood-bodied Iveco 2063 is seen at the Wibsey terminus of Yorkshire Rider service 845 on 19 April 1990.

RETRENCHMENT AT YORK

Coming quickly on the heels of West Yorkshire's departure from the North of England Travel Group was a massive shake-up in April of the fleets of the remaining subsidiaries during which no fewer than 36 vehicles were withdrawn and offered for sale. Harrogate & District removed from service a Leyland National I and 3 Leyland National 2s, all of which except for one of the latter were sold to the associated AJS companies within the South of England Travel Group whilst Challenger withdrew their former London DMS-type Fleetline. Within days of its revenue-earning duties ending, this bus which was registered GHV1N lost its identity in favour of a 'new' number (KWU410N), its original mark being temporarily transferred to York City & District's Ford Transit pick-up truck D495KAG. Obviously in preparation for its ultimate sale, the ailing York City & District made drastic cuts to its fleet by withdrawing no fewer than 30 vehicles of which 25 were Bristol VRTs and the remaining 5 were short Leyland Nationals. Two of the latter were destined to join the Alan Stephenson's South of England Travel Group whilst 3 of the VRTs - including the two open-top examples - passed to Guide Friday for continued use in York. One VRT was reansferred to Harrogate Independent Travel (Challenger) whilst 20 were sold to Cambus of Cambridge for operation in their own and associated Viscount fleets. Keighley & District fared much better than the previously mentioned companies with only one Bristol VRT being removed from service. In addition to this large number of departures, a general reshuffle of many of the remaining vehicles took place at this same time with York City & District gaining 6 Leyland Lynx, 2 dual purpose Leopards and 4 Olympians - 2 of which were coach-seated - from Harrogate & District in exchange for 2 Olympians and 4 Leyland National 2s. Yorkshire Coastliner transferred 2 of its dual purpose-seated Olympians to

Harrogate & District and one of its Leopards to York City, gaining in their place 2 dual purpose Olympians from York and a Leopard from Harrogate and at the end of the month, following the arrival of their new Tigers, they withdrew five Leopards which were then immediately sold. Following all these comings and goings, York City & District no longer operated any Bristol VRTs or Leyland Nationals, although one of the latter (1011), despite its pending departure, was still in daily use early in June. Similarly, a number of York & Harrogate's other Leyland Nationals withdrawn 'on paper' survived in service on borrowed time for a few more weeks before running their final journeys at the end of April or early May.

To compensate for the departure of some of these vehicles, Harrogate & District received four new Leyland Lynxes in April, these differing from their predecessors in having dual purpose-type seating for 47 passengers, and a further three new Reeve Burgess-bodied dual purpose 31-seat Renault S75s, whilst Yorkshire Coastliner took delivery of their five new Plaxton Paramount-bodied Leyland Tigers. Of the latter, although all were received in Coastliner's cream & blue livery, only three at first carried their owner's fleet names, the remaining pair being unlettered except for their legal requirements. Target Travel at York almost doubled their fleet when, on 5 April they placed in service eight new Reeve Burgess-bodied 23-seat Renault S56s plus an identical vehicle which had previously

Right : One of the two former York City & District open-top Bristol VRTs purchased by Guide Friday for use on their York Tour, DWU839H had already received its new owner's cream & green livery when photographed on a wet day in June 1990.

Below : One of the Leyland Lynx buses transferred from Harrogate & District to York City & District in April 1990, 25 climbs Sattion Rise, York on its way to Chapelfields on local city service 7 on 2 June 1990.

Below right : York City & District Leyland National 1521 seen here in Rougier Street, York in March 1989 was a year later transferred to the Harrogate & District fleet in which it was numbered 340.   (J.Whitmore)

been a demonstrator. At first these new additions ran with temporary York City & District legal ownership panels until their own incesase in operators discs was authorised, but by the end of the month all had been 'officially' transferred to the Target fleet. As mentioned earlier, Harrogate Independent Travel had further increased its fleet by the addition of a Bristol VRT from York City & District and at around this same time, Leopard AEG984A lost its Northern Rose blue colour scheme in favour of Challenger's all-over white.

During April 1990, the fleets of Harrogate & District, York City & District and Yorkshire Coastliner were all renumbered into individual series' and each was done in a most haphazard fashion. Harrogate & District made a feeble attempt to marry its fleet numbers with some of the digits in the registration number of each vehicle and numbered its mini and midibuses between 245 and 295 (with gaps); its double deckers between 310 and 322 (again with gaps) and its single deck Leyland Nationals and Lynxes between 332 and 381. York City & District and Yorkshire Coastliner similarly attempted to reflect registration numbers in their fleet numbers but started at 3 and 424 respectively.

One of Harrogate & Dsitrict's new dual purpose-seated Leyland Lynx buses, 383, is seen here in its home town bus station on 14 April 1990 before taking up its duties on the prestigious 36 service to Leeds. (J.Whitmore)

Yorkshire Coastliner Plaxton Paramount-bodied Leyland Tiger 434 resting here in Central Bus Station, Leeds following its arrival from Scarborough had still to receive its fleet names when caught by the camera on 19 May 1990.

Above : Target Travel Renault S56 minibus G447LKW was originally a demonstration vehicle for its coachbuilder, Reeve Burgess. In full Target livery, it approaches York railway station on 2 June 1990 enroute to Foxwood Lane on service 50.

Above : Purchased new in January 1990 by Harrogate Independent Travel (Challenger), Reeve Burgess-bodied Renault S56 G327MUA leaves Harrogate bus station on route 7 to Hornbeam Park on 22 May 1990.

Repainted in Keighley & District's new chinchilla & red livery, Leyland National 283 had recently been renumbered from 1517, its new fleet number vinyl having a red background. Here it turns from Cavendish Street, Keighley into Lawkholme Crescent on its way to the bus station on a local town service on 10 May 1990.

The most dramatic news of the month was however that relating to York City & District's operations. Quite unbelievably, a decision was taken to withdraw Sunday services on all routes and to reduce the Monday to Saturday frequencies in the evenings with effect from 8 April. Such drastic measures were believed to be necessary to reduce costs within the company, which it appeared was not nearly as healthy as it seemed to be on the surface. In order to plug the massive gap left in the city, Target Travel introduced Sunday services between Wiggington and Dringhouses (1B); Heslington and Chapel Fields (7A), Rawcliffe and Fulford (30/1) and Strensall and Beckfield Lane (32/3), although each of these ran only hourly, and independents Hirst; Hutchinson; Reliance and Acomb Link also stepped in the fill the breach on Sundays with assistance from North Yorkshire County Council and York City Council to ensure that at least some public transport was available for local residents and tourists in the city, and in addition, undertook some local daytime services on weekdays. Target also began a new Monday - Saturday minibus service on 9 April from Clifton Moor to Bishopthorpe and Keble Park, numbering this 18 (or 18A for journeys diverted via the city's Technical College) whilst Reynard Buses increased their presence in the city with the introduction of further Monday to Saturday services. Another feature of this hugh shake-up in York was the revision of several of York City's existing Monday to Saturday services, a number of which from 9 April either operated via revised routes or had their terminal points altered. Coinciding with their massive withdrawal of services at the end of the first week of April, York City & District additionally implemented a fares increase under which the cost of some journeys went up by a staggering 25%. The cost of York pensioners passes was also increased to £28 per year, entitling holders to pay a maximum fare of 25p on any single journey within the city and to certain places beyond the boundary. Despite being the joint operators of certain services, Yorkshire Coastliner and York City & District appeared to be unable to get their act together when on Good Friday (13 April), the former operated a Sunday service on their 843 Leeds - York - Scarborough service whilst York City & District provided a Saturday service on the 844 route from Leeds to York !

Across in Harrogate, Challenger began two new services on 9 April, one, the 22 to Beckwith Knowle Industrial Estate with six return journeys each day, Monday to Friday, the other, numbered 24 to York with four return journeys each day, Monday to Saturday increasing to eight per day from 28 July to 4 September. On the other hand, Keighley & District withdrew their Monday, Tuesday, Thursday and Friday journeys on the 500 service from Hebden Bridge to Keighley with effect from 16 April leaving this operated jointly by Abbeyways and Yorkshire Rider on Wednesdays, Saturdays and Sundays only.

Although Yorkshire Rider had their own well-equipped repair workshops at Kirkstall Road, Leeds, several of their

former West Yorkshire vehicles visited Premier Engineering at Harrogate to receive attention during April, thus for the time being at least, continuing to maintain links between the company's former buses and their familiar surrounds.

A surprise arrival early in May was that of a County Bus & Coach Co. ECW-bodied Leyland Olympian at Keighley. Being received on the 3rd of that month, it wore the old London Country North East two-tone green & white livery and was notable in being the first double decker to receive

Above : One of York City & District's main competitors is local independent Reynard Buses whose NCME-bodied Renault F363BUA with Yorbus fleet name is seen passing the city's railway station on 2 June 1990 enroute to South Bank on service 13.

Below : Another competitor to York City & District, albeit on a small scale is Acomb Link whose ex.Merthyr Tydfil East Lancs-bodied Leyland Leopard GHB176J pulls away from Station Rise on the service to Foxwood on 6 June 1990.

Yorkshire Rider 1552, an ex.West Yorkshire red & cream-liveried Duple dual purpose-bodied Leyland Leopard having arrived from Bradford on the 653 service rests in Harrogate bus station on 22 May 1990 alongside Harrogate & District 321, a dual purpose-seated Olympian recently transferred from Yorkshire Coastliner.

Hired by Keighley & District from County Bus & Coach Co. of Harlow, an AJS South of England Travel Group subsidiary, for evaluation in May 1990, ECW-bodied Leyland Olympian LR69 is seen here in its London Country North East livery - albeit with Keighley & District fleet names and logos - in Keighley bus station on 23 May. Following its purchase a few days later it was immediately repainted into Keighley's standard chinchilla & red colours.

Then recently acquired from County Bus & Coach Co., Keighley & District ECW-bodied Olympian 376 (B265LPH) had the green areas of its former owner's livery repainted red before taking up its duties in Yorkshire. With its new operator's fleet names and logos added, it hurries towards Keighley from Cross Roads on a 665 journey to Bradford on 23 June 1990.

this colour scheme when it was introduced in 1986. Hired for evaluation purposes, it entered service with Keighley & District on 11 May with K & D vinyl fleet names and logos but still retaining its County Bus fleet number LR69 and HA (Harlow) depot code and was used on a variety of services including those running to Bradford. Being higher than Keighley & District's own Olympians prevented it from passing under the railway bridge in Park Lane, Keighley but following clearance tests it was found suitable for use on the Skipton service on which there was also a low bridge. Obviously regarded as being successful following its trials, it was purchased before the end of May along with six further buses of this same type, the first of which travelled north on 17 May. This (LR65) arrived wearing the new cream & green livery of County Bus & Coach Co. and rather than repaint it into chinchilla & red, it instead retained its cream areas and had its green repainted red to give it the same appearance as Keighley's coach-seated Olympians which had not yet succumbed to the new fleet colours. In this guise and numbered 65, it entered service in its new home on 29 May and was joined a few days later by another Olympian (LR68) which was similarly treated. 65 had by this time been renumbered 376 however to bring it in line with the rest of the Keighley fleet. In the meantime, LR69 had lost its original owner's two-tone green & white colour scheme in favour of Keighley & District's chinchilla & red livery and had been renumbered 380. The arrival of these acquired double deckers allowed the withdrawal of a similar number of Bristol VRTs and Plaxton-bodied dual purpose Leyland Leopard 221 which ran its final journey on 5 June.

Keighley & District's Northern Rose coaching operation which had almost ceased to exist in 1989 was reactivated at the start of the 1990 summer season, but unbelievably comprised only one coach, 244, a Plaxton Paramount-bodied Leyland Tiger. This still wore its Northern Rose livery and had its fare collection system removed following its use as a dual purpose vehicle during 1989 and the winter of 89/90.

Following intervention by the Traffic Commissioners, Pinnacle Coaches of Crosshills withdrew their 766 service on 13 May whilst on the following day Steels Coaches of Addingham introduced new competition to Keighley & District when they began a new local service in the Silsden area which also served Airedale Hospital.

Target Travel, who had now fitted all their fleet with new white on green destination blinds were granted a new licence in their own name for their York city service 50 which had previously been held in the name of B.C.Gallier t/a Premier Coaches despite Target's change of ownership earlier in the year, and also started a new service on 29 May from York to Stamford Bridge. Operating on Mondays to Saturdays, direct journeys were numbered 48X whilst those serving Dunnington were numbered 48 and both were obviously designed to attack Reynard Buses in retaliation for their incursion on York City & District's city services. Added to Target's fleet for operation on this new route was a dual purpose-seated NCME-bodied Renault S56 (E575ANE) transferred from Harrogate Independent Travel at the end of May which ironically had previously operated for Reynard Pullman. Replacing this at Harrogate was a Reeve Burgess-

Passing Keighley bus station on its owner's competitive service to Skipton on 11 October 1989 is Pinnacle Coaches Talbot Tri-axle minibus E651KCW. This service along with all the others operated by Pinnacle in competition with Keighley & District has now been withdrawn following the revocation of their operator's licence by the Traffic Commissioners.

bodied 25-seat Iveco which had been acquired a few weeks earlier from Reeve Burgess following use in their demonstration fleet. It was immediately placed in service still wearing the Plaxton Group's corporate exhibition livery of white, red & blue which incorporated the outline of a bird on each side of its body. Meanwhile, Challenger's withdrawn ex.London Fleetline and Caetano-bodied Bedford YMT were both moved to the yard behind Grove Park depot, Harrogate for storage pending their sale.

Continuing their practise of repainting a vehicle into the livery of each of their former constituent members, Yorkshire Rider similarly afforded this privilege to one of their recently-acquired West Yorkshire buses, Leeds-based Leyland Olympian 5187. This was repainted into Tilling red & cream complete with traditional 'West Yorkshire' gold underlined fleet names early in May and in similar fashion to other buses in the Rider fleet which had been given the colours of their original constituent owners, it was adorned with the legend 'Yorkshire Rider Building on a Great Future' in gold lettering on its upper panels on each side. Surprisingly, a second Olympian was similarly treated towards the end of June when Bradford depot's 5199 was repainted in an identical manner. At around this same time Yorkshire Coastliner transformed one of its inherited Leyland Leopards and an Olympian by repainting them into its new blue & cream colours and fitting them with the restyled Coastliner names and logos.

Properties continued to feature in the news with the lease of Harrogate bus station being further extended to enable it to remain in use until at least September 1990, thus deferring the fateful day when buses would be relegated to picking up and setting down passengers in the town's busy

streets. Work on the new depot at Manse Lane, Knaresborough was progressing more slowly than had been intended and a prefabricated building purchased for erection on this site was temporarily being stored in a dismantled state on the land behind York depot. Indeed, when Manse Lane was brought into use on 31 May, the only building at this new depot was a Portakabin ! Meanwhile, Harrogate & District's minibus fleet had moved to the Dairy Crest premises at Camwal Road, Starbeck on 20 May and thus following the departure of the midibuses and conventional-sized vehicles to Knaresborough, the doors of Grove Park depot at Harrogate were closed for the last time. The six withdrawn vehicles (2 Challenger and 4 Keighley & District) stored at Grove Park at that time were moved to the old chassis shop at Myrtle Road which although sold had not yet been demolished and was 'available' short term.

The planning application to demolish Grassington depot and bus station and replace it with residential dwellings was refused by the National Parks Committee on the grounds that due to alternative garaging and picking up points having not yet been found, the proposed development was both premature and unacceptable. Keighley & District's new head office in the town, at 20 Devonshire Street, became functional early in April although at Skipton, the company's enquiry office still remained incognito possibly due to the fact that it was still to be finalised whether or not this was to carry the name 'Craven Bus'. Despite the depot in Skipton being long gone, three Keighley & District buses were still outstationed in the town each night residing at the Cattle Market. At Otley, the former depot in Bondgate was now converted to a Kwik Fit Motorists Centre whilst that at Roseville Road, Leeds had still to be occupied by its new owner, Barr & Wallace Arnold Trust. At Hammerton Street, Bradford, following the collapse of its sale, the depot was placed back on the market. The long running saga of the proposed closure of the bus station at Wetherby continued and following more complaints and a petition by residents of that town, West Yorkshire PTA stepped in. After offering funding to Techno, the new owners of the site, agreement was reached to the effect that a new bus station would be incorporated in the future redevelopment. Buses were however no longer housed overnight at Wetherby following the opening of Harrogate & District's new premises at Manse Lane, Knaresborough.

Originally an NCME demonstrator and later purchased by Reynard Pullman of York, NCME-bodied Renault E575ANE passed to Harrogate Independent Travel with Reynard's operations in that area in January 1990. Transferred to Target Travel, York in May 1990, it is seen here at Osbaldwick in its new owner's cream & green livery enroute to York on 6 June 1990 on Target's new route from Stamford Bridge.

Only four Leyland Leopards now remain in the York City & District fleet. One of these, 53, which still carries NBC poppy red & white livery, leaves York railway station on a journey to Leeds on service 844 on 6 June 1990.

Right : Two former West Yorkshire Road Car Co. Leyland Olympians have been repainted in their original livery by Yorkshire Rider under their commemorative policy. The second of these, 5199 is seen leaving Bradford Interchange at the start of its journey to Ilkley on service 650 on 2 July 1990.

Below right : Wearing a plain white colour scheme in preparation for an all-over advertising livery, York City & District's dual purpose-seated former Coastliner Olympian 90 approaches Rougier Street, York whilst working a city service on 2 June 1990.

Fewer changes were made to the fleets of the North of England Travel Group's subsidiaries during May and apart from those already recorded at Keighley, the only other changes were the withdrawal of Challenger's Caetano-bodied Bedford coach and its replacement on the 15th of the month by a dual purpose Plaxton-bodied Leyland Leopard transferred from Yorkshire Coastliner. Withdrawn short Leyland National 1010 was despatched on loan to Rover Coaches of Worcester who also purchased the former Challenger Bedford and two of the other Leyland Nationals sold for scrap following their withdrawal in April were snapped up by the Caldaire Group for service in their United Automobile Services fleet.

Apart from the West Yorkshire vehicles transferred to Yorkshire Rider depots at Kinsley, Halifax and Huddersfield on or before the total absorption of the former company on 1 April, the remainder continued to operate in the Leeds and Bradford areas, albeit often on unfamiliar services. The Leyland Nationals which had moved to Huddersfield proved distinctly unpopular with crews however and by early June four of the fourteen transferred had still to enter service in their new surrounds. The first former West Yorkshire vehicle to be reallocated after 1 April was Olympian 5190 which, after receiving Yorkshire Rider livery was moved from Bradford to Todmorden on 25 May. It did not stay long in its new home along the Calder Valley however and was moved to Halifax on 14 June - still with YR Todmorden fleet names !

As had been expected, York City & District and Target Travel were both offered for sale during the final week of June and immediately attracted attention from Reynard Buses; Yorkshire Rider and more surprisingly, Thames Transit. Although each company was to be sold separately, it made sense that both should pass to the same buyer in view of their close operating liason and the former West Yorkshire empire was further fragmented. Yorkshire Coastliner and its operations however were surprisingly not included in the sale and was to be retained as a member of the North of England Travel Group despite now being many miles from any of the three remaining Group companies. Coastliner's Olympians were now starting to receive the new-style blue & cream livery in place of their former, and more attractive, two-tone blue & white colour scheme and carried their new fleet name and logo on the between decks panels on each side.

Following the protracted battle between Harrogate & District and Harrogate District Council in respect of picking up and setting down points in Knaresborough, the town's bus station was surprisingly reopened on 1 July and used by all routes serving the town, including those of Harrogate Independent Travel.

To reduce Keighley & District's Bristol VRT fleet even further, an order was placed for six new NCME-bodied Leyland Olympians for delivery in September, but in the

event these began to arrive during the final days of June and were despatched to the paint shop before eventually being licenced for service. Meanwhile, at this same time the company began to experiment in an attempt to improve their uninspiring chinchilla & red colour scheme and treated three of their original ECW-bodied Olympians to different revised liveries which on two incorporated red window frames to both decks and the third to red upper deck panels. This greatly improved their appearance and it will be interested to see which of these - if any - eventually becomes standard.

Former West Yorkshire Duple-bodied dual purpose Leyland Leopard was repainted in an all-over buttermilk livery with black relief by its new owner, Yorkshire Rider. Pictured here entering Bradford Interchange on 2 July 1990, it was on that day being employed on the Harrogate service.

Resting in their home depot on 26 June are Keighley & District Olympians 367 and 354, both of which are painted in experimental liveries. The variations between the two can be seen with 367 having a red band above its lower deck windows and thin blue line below and 354 having its blue line above its red skirt. A third trial livery incorporated red upper deck panels and grey upper deck window frames.

Left : Harrogate & District's Reeve Burgess-bodied midibus 294 awaits its passengers in Harrogate bus station before leaving on a journey to Tadcaster on 14 April 1990. (J.Whitmore)

Below left : Two of York City & District's Iveco minibuses - Robin Hood-bodied 160 and Pheonix-bodied 210 are seen on a wet June day in 1990 after arriving at the Station Rise, York terminus of city service 9.

Thus, in the space of less than three years since its return from the National Bus Company to the private sector, West Yorkshire Road Car Co. Ltd. has been divided, restructured and resold. Only a handful of the old company's properties are still being used for their intended purpose and before long, even the famous Tilling red & cream livery will have become but a memory. The company's well-known name has disappeared completely and of the remaining fragmented parts of this once-mighty company, now a mere shadow of its former self, it seems highly unlikely that the North of England Travel Group will retain Harrogate & District and the more recently acquired Harrogate Independent Travel beyond a further twelve months. How long Yorkshire Coastliner and Keighley & District will survive is a matter of speculation and only the fullness of time will provide the answer. Whatever the future however, West Yorkshire's long and proud history will always be remembered with affection despite its abrupt and undignified end.

Back cover :

Left column, top to bottom :

Despite wearing Yorkshire Rider Huddersfield livery, Roe-bodied Leyland Atlantean 6337 was officially transferred to the subsidiary West Yorkshire fleet as confirmed by the red legal lettering panel behind the front wheel. It is seen here on 12 January 1990 leaving Vicar Lane bus station, Leeds enroute to Whinmoor on service 795.

Painted in Harrogate Independent Travel's all-white livery, Plaxton-bodied Leyland Leopard DNW837T was transferred to that company from York City & District in whose fleet it was numbered 2565. It is seen here passing through Starbeck on its way to Ripon on 22 May 1990.

One of a pair of Plaxton Derwent dual purpose-bodied Leyland Leopards transferred from Yorkshire Rider Halifax to West Yorkshire, 8516 resplendent in the livery of its new owner approaches Bradford Interchange on an X1 journey from Otley on 15 September 1989.

Numerically the first of Yorkshire Coastliner's new Plaxton Paramount-bodied Leyland Tigers, 431 hurries through the outskirts of York on its way to Malton on an 843 journey early in June 1990.

Right column, top to bottom :

Keighley & District adopted a Tilling red livery with grey band for its Bristol VRTs rather than the new standard chinchilla & red colour scheme. Freshly-repainted 313, seen here operating a Keighley town service on 23 May 1990 had also received a new-style fleet name.

York City & District's new livery of blue & cream is shown to good effect on former Coastliner Olympian 1857 as it leaves Vicar Lane bus station, Leeds on 30 March 1990 at the start of its long journey to Scarborough on service 843.

One of Target Travel's Reeve Burgess-bodied Renault S56s, G193NWY travels along Station Road, York on its was to Foxwood Lane on 2 June 1990.

Former Yorkshire Coastliner dual purpose Leyland Olympian 321 illustrates Harrogate & Districts new red & cream livery as its rests in the town's threatened bus station on 22 May 1990 after completing a schools contract duty.